My Family's
Irish And Spanish Pioneers
Of Custer County, Montana
And Leavenworth County, Kansas
And Their Descendants

My Family's
Irish And Spanish Pioneers
Of Custer County, Montana
And Leavenworth County, Kansas
And Their Descendants

Richard Baskas

To order additional copies of this book, contact:
Xlibris Corporation
1-888-795-4274
www.Xlibris.com
Orders@Xlibris.com
76010

Contents

Researcher: Richard S. Baskas
Contributors: Margaret K. "M.K." Baskas
    and (Dr.) Leger Brosnahan

Researcher: Richard S. Baskas

Researcher: Richard S. Baskas
Contributors: James "Jim" A. Baskas, John "Buddy" Baskas;
    Margaret K. "M.K." Baskas and (Dr.) Leger Brosnahan

Researcher: Richard S. Baskas
Contributors: Margaret K. "M.K."Baskas, James "Jim" A. Baskas,
    Linda Glynn-Hutchinson, (Dr.) Leger Brosnahan

Researcher: Richard S. Baskas

Researcher: Richard S. Baskas

CHAPTER I

BASKAS

Researcher
Richard S. Baskas

Contributors
James "Jim" A. Baskas; Patrick Baskas; Kathy Baskas-Goldak

It was 30 May 1854 and President Franklin Pierce had signed the Kansas-Nebraska bill opening the Kansas Territory for settlement. Most of Kansas' growth started with the passing and enactment of the Homestead Law, which was passed in 1862 and became effective on 1 January 1863. This bill allowed people in Kansas and Nebraska to decide for themselves whether or not to allow slavery within their borders. The act served to repeal the Missouri Compromise of 1820 which prohibited slavery north of latitude 36 degrees and 30 minutes. The Act infuriated many in the North who considered the Compromise to be a long-standing binding agreement. After the Act was passed, pro-slavery supporters rushed in to settle Kansas to affect the outcome of the first election held there after the law went into effect. Pro-slavery settlers carried the election but were charged with fraud by anti-slavery, and the results were not accepted by them. The anti-slavery settlers held another election; however pro-slavery settlers refused to vote. This resulted in the establishment of two opposing legislatures within the Kansas territory. Violence soon erupted, with the anti-slavery forced led by John Brown. The territory became "Bleeding Kansas" as the death toll rose. President Pierce, in support of the pro-slavery settlers, sent in Federal troops to stop the violence and disperse the anti-legislature. Another election was called. Once again pro-slavery supporters won and once again they were charged with election fraud. As a result, Congress did not recognize the constitution adopted by the pro-slavery settlers and Kansas was not allowed to become a state. Eventually, anti-slavery settlers outnumbered pro-slavery settlers and a new constitution was drawn up. On 29 January 1861, just before the start of the Civil War, Kansas was admitted to the Union as a free state.

The Act offered "free" land to those who would live on and cultivate a tract. In order to make a claim, the individual had to (1) be 21 years of age or head of a family, (2) be a United States citizen or have declared intention to become one, (3) not already own 320 acres of land, (4) not abandon land owned by him in the same state or territory, and (5) intend to use the homestead for himself and his family. Millions of land grants and patents were issued by the federal government and by the original thirteen colonies and several states. These records include application files and the patents themselves. Homestead files have some family info and maybe naturalization papers. Before 4 July 1836, the president of the United States signed land patents. After this date, Congress authorized the president to appoint a secretary to sign the president's name on patents.

Research on our family history began about 1997 when I when to visit my grandmother's stone at Mount Calvary Cemetery in Lansing where the Baskas pioneers and a few of their children are buried. Through the years of researching this branch, which included many discussions among many immediate family members, I found that not much was ever passed down to the generations. I may have heard a few stories but none that went back far enough. Mount Calvary has records of two plots that belonged to one of the pioneers and another of some of their children. One plot has a bigger stone, of the pioneers: Joseph Baskas, and his wife, Johanna McMahon, and their daughter, Mary. Surrounding this stone are 4 smaller stones (flush to the ground): Mary, Marie (Baskas) DeWoody, Michael Glynn and his wife, Elizabeth Baskas. Another plot has one big stone: Annie (wife of Frank Baskas, son of pioneers), Thomas Killalay (possible brother of Annie) and Mary J. (wife of George Taylor). After exhausting what the cemetery office had in their files, I started with the Leavenworth Library which provided census and many other records that helped clarify the relationships. From here, I ended up practically exhausting every building in town trying to find what I could.

Mount Calvary records list Joseph Baskas as being born on 25 December **1831** in Madrid, Spain. Census records show Joseph immigrating in **1841**, then to possibly Missouri and then to Kansas.

KICKAPOO, KANSAS

The earliest official records that is known of the Baskas family is the **1860**, Kickapoo, Kansas Census that shows Joseph *Basket* from Spain, living in the 2nd Ward of Leavenworth City aged 28 years, therefore, he was born about **1832**, working as a grocer with 400 acres. On 3 September, Joseph *Bascus* was naturalized in Leavenworth, age 29, therefore, born about **1831**. **1862**, 9 November, *Joseph Baschus* and *Joanna McMahon* were married at the Immaculate Conception Church in Leavenworth by Rev. Theodore Heimann, with Patrick O'Brien and Mary Loughlin as witnesses. Kansas census shows she immigrated to an unknown place, then to Canada, then on to Kansas. Johanna was born on 10 November **1844** in County Claire, Ireland. **1865**, Kickapoo census shows Joseph with 385 acres, and Johanna, age 27, born about 1838 in Ireland. They have a family of four: Frank, Mary, Anthony and Joseph. According to four of the pioneer's children's baptismals, there are four McMahon's who were sponsors: *Patrick McMan* in 20 August **1865**, *Maggie McMahon* sponsored on 17 May **1868**, *Mary McMahon* in 18 April **1869**, and *Bridget McMahon* in 13 May **1871**. It's unclear their relationships to us. Family had mentioned that Joseph had owned land in Kickapoo and Lowemont, but research at Leavenworth courthouse and Leavenworth Public Library show no record of any Baskas (or variations of the name) having owned any land there. An **1875** Kickapoo census shows the family still here. Family mentions that Monsignor Harvey, who resided at IMAC years ago, mentioned that the Baskas family was the first of the church, unknown of this meaning.

LEAVENWORTH, KANSAS

By **1890**, Joseph moved into Leavenworth where he and his family lived at 1023 North 5th Street. His sons were miners while he owned and ran his grocer business at 1025 North 5th until he retired in 1900. The family stayed here until Joseph's death, and his son, Frank, continued living there until **1904**. **1892**, 23 May, Joseph bought a piece of cemetery property at Mt. Calvary on lot 19, block 1 and section 2. **1902**, 18 April, Johanna died in Leavenworth. According to family, after Johanna died, Joseph hired a maid (name unknown) to live with him and take care of him, later leaving money to her when he would die. This caused a family feud and his family ended up not having anything to do with him. **1903**, 5 November, Joseph died in Leavenworth at his daughter's house of Elizabeth Glynn at 570 Second Street. Both had their funerals from Sacred Heart to Mt. Calvary Cemetery. On 20 December 1999, Joseph was proven as a *TERRITORIAL PIONEER OF KANSAS* by R.S. Baskas which was later published in *THE FORGOTTEN SETTLERS OF KANSAS*, Volume 24, by the Kansas Council of Genealogical Societies, Inc. 2001. The Baskas family history was published (by R.S. Baskas) in the Leavenworth Times, 27 June 2004 for the town's anniversary (there are a few mistakes done by the newspaper personnel). Because of all the activity that went on in the 400 Pawnee house since Daniel and Margaret Pike first bought it and raised their family (their daughter married John Baskas), myself and my father, Jim Baskas, did what could be done to get a historical plaque put up for the house. Unfortunately, not enough proof or historical history was able to be provided and so the Carroll Mansion was unable to provide a plaque.

Joseph Baskas and Johanna McMahon:

Frank Joseph Baskas m. Annie Marie Killilay
Mary C. Baskas
Anthony Baskas m. Ella
Joseph "Windy" Jr. Baskas
Jennie/Jane Baskas m. John Perry
James Baskas
Elizabeth Baskas m. Michael F. Glynn
William Baskas
J.W. (Joseph William?) Baskas m. Violet McNeil
Katherine Baskas
John Burke Baskas m. Margaret Pike-Becker
Rose Baskas m. Kearney

CHAPTER II

KANELLY

Researcher
Richard S. Baskas

Contributor
(Dr.) Leger Brosnahan

MIDDLETON, CORK COUNTY, IRELAND (<1857)

According to cemetery records at Mt. Calvary in Lansing, Kansas and baptismal records of the first generation children, the Kanelly's were from *Midleton, Cork County, Ireland.* There is a Middletown, Cork County, Ireland but unsure if this is it. Through much of this research, the last name has been seen as *Kneally, Keley, Connely, Kaennaelly, Kanelly,* and *Kenley.* To this date, there are definitely three members of this family positively found, *Jim Connely, Margaret Josephine Kanelly* and *Kate Kaennaelly.* According to stories, there are supposed to be more members. Years later, Kanelly and Roache descendants provided a document with what could be the parents of the immigrants to Leavenworth, *Kneally (?) and (Lady) Margaret O'Neal (?).* The story of my late Aunt Eileen, granddaughter of Margaret, is that Margaret immigrated with two or three of her brothers, either to Ellis Island, New York or to possibly Philadelphia, Pennsylvania. Her brothers were to make sure that she made the trip okay before two of them returned back to Ireland, but one was to stay.

Kneally (?) and (Lady) Margaret O'Neal (?):

... ONE BROTHER, JIM CONNELY, BILLINGS, MONTANA ... is the only mention of a brother, from Margaret Josephine's obituary of 1933.

MARGARET JOSEPHINE KANELLY, according to cemetery records, b. 28 May **1857,**

> Midleton, Cork County, Ireland; According to Aunt Eileen the story begins that Margaret was living in Ireland when her future first husband, Michael Roache, was visiting his family there and happened to meet her there. He had taken leave, while serving in the Civil War, and went back to Ireland to see his family, where he met Margaret. Roache descendants described her as a beautiful 15-year-old, who probably never had shoes on before. Michael had decided that he would have her sent to Leavenworth and would marry her there. Kansas Census shows her immigrating between **1871** and **1874.** During my visit to my Aunt Eileen, just before she passed on, she had mentioned Margaret having immigrated with Mrs. Margaret Kelly, Mrs. Igoe (Eileen even spelled the last name!) and a young priest, Bernard S. Kelly, who would later become Monsignor Kelly of the Immaculate Conception Catholic Church in Leavenworth, Kansas.

KATE KEANNEALLY, was born 2 February **1867** in *North Ireland,* from Kansas census and her obituary. Her last name spelled according to Roache papers.

FORT LEAVENWORTH, KANSAS

Roache descendants mentioned that *Jim Connely* was living in Leavenworth when he was sent to Montana in **1879** to work on the Roache family ranch while Michael was working at the post. Kansas Census mentions Kate having already been in the states for 20 years and so her immigration date would probably be about **1880.** This could be when she and Margaret came to the states together? It's clear that Catherine wasn't born until after Margaret went back to Ireland. It had been rumored that when Margaret

Josephine Kanelly-Roache returned to the states with her daughter, Nell, for a short absence from her husband, she apparently also came back with a sibling, her sister, Catherine. Catherine apparently hadn't been born yet.

Jim Connely may have come back to Leavenworth with his sister as there is a *James Connely* who was a witness to a baptismal of our James Roche on 27 January **1884** in Leavenworth. Margaret's granddaughter (Munnie's daughter, Helen Rose Mottin-Brosnahan) Sammie Vaughn, Helen's daughter, had written a paper for her school based on our family history:

> *And she* [Margaret] *was a beautiful little fifteen year old, who had never had shoes on probably. And they* [Margaret and Michael] *got married. And they came . . .*

I've decided to put this part of the story in this branch, due to overwhelming evidence I've found. I had heard the story many times from my father as he remembered it as a child. He remembered playing in this trunk, which was a little bigger than he where it was probably in the basement of his older brother's (Buddy) house. The trunk wouldn't be heard of for some time until the day that Buddy would pass on. My father had mentioned about the trunk to his niece, Kathy, Buddy's daughter. The truck was found in the basement and passed on to my father. My father had examined the insides to see what had accumulated over the years. One of the most surprising items were two pictures of what was to be my great-grandmother, Margaret Josephine Kanelly. My father contacted a few of his brothers and it appeared that agreed that it was her. After thinking about it, I had decided that I wanted to examine it to determine if there were any markings throughout it, company logos, etc. to determine where it was manufactured. I went back to Leavenworth and examined the trunk thoroughly, including what was inside. My stepmother, M.K., was also in town and she shared another story. She remembered the trunk being at her mother's house in the closet top shelf at the Pawnee house, but never used it as she always used suitcases. So why have the trunk in the first place? Grandma's mother passed on at that house on 400 Pawnee. Hence the reason I believe the trunk may have belonged to Grandma Kanelly.

Aunt Eileen mentioned that Margaret traveled the Missouri River to meet with her husband who was stationed at Fort Leavenworth. One mystery of this is that possibly she immigrated to New Orleans and used a steamship going north. If she had emigrated from the east, why travel by water, why not via Fort Leavenworth Bridge? On her way there, either she thought that she was supposed to go to St. Joseph, Missouri or the people she was with on the boat on the river thought that she was going to St. Joseph's. One of the men there mentioned that she wouldn't be able to enter the fort and so he invited her to stay at 400 Pawnee, which was supposed to have been a tavern at the time. Supposedly, up until her marriage with him, she never knew he was in the military.

CHAPTER III

ROACHE

Researcher
Richard S. Baskas

Contributor
(Dr.) Leger Brosnahan

IRELAND (<1834)

It wasn't realized that Margaret was married twice until research revealed a Kansas census showing that some of her previous children had the last name of *Roache* and was born and lived in Montana. Research in Custor County, Montana revealed that MICHAEL (ROMANUS/DE LA ROCHE?) may have been born in Ireland about **1834** as his military records may mention. His descendants mentioned that he may be a descendant from the *de la Roche* family, who were originally from France who may have migrated to Spain and then to Ireland before coming to the United States. During this time in Ireland, the army was English and the Irish hated them bitterly. Because he met Margaret in Ireland, it's a pretty good assumption that he was from about the same area as she where he met here. Michael's father may have already arrived or been born in New York before Michael was born. Michael apparently spent some time in an orphanage in New York until he was 15, when he ran away to the shipyards. The earliest information regarding Michael and Margaret was first compiled from an interview with Margaret's granddaughter (Munnie's daughter, Helen Rose Mottin-Brosnahan) by Sammie Vaughn, Helen's daughter:

> (Helen) *Monnie's father came from Ireland, where the army was English, and the Irish hated them bitterly . . . But he came over here and for whatever reason—what would he be prepared to do outside of common labor—he joined the army.*

> (Helen) *And he did well in the army and I think he was a technical sergeant. something like that. At any rate, when he was thirty years old, he went, he had a year's furlough, or a long furlough of some kind, and he went home to Ireland, he had saved . . . his money and oh he was a credit to the twon and a great fellow. And she [Margaret] was a beautiful little fifteen year old, who had never had shoes on probably. And they got married. And they came . . .*

> (Sammie) *Did they get married over there [Ireland]?*

> (Helen) *Yes. And no, Mother told me . . . no,*

> (Sammie) *Marf has some story of a marriage certificate but I forgot to look at it.*

> (Helen) *But they didn't get married there. He came back and just sent for her.*

> (Sammie) *Yes, that's right.*

> (Helen) *And she came out here and they were married at the Cathedral in north Leavenworth.*

> (Sammie) *That's right.*

> (Helen) *And she discovered that he was in the army. And this was frightful.*

> (Sammie) *Strange, how does he keep a thing like that from her?*

(Helen) *He's thirty years old and he's a severe reglious type of Irishman and she has never kept house or done a living thing and she's only fifteen years old and pretty soon—ah, I don't remember whether—she got sick, I think, and had pneumonia, and they took her in to St. John's hospital and the sisters nursed her. And when she got well she refused absolutely to go back to her husband. She was not going to have any part of him. And so the sisters said, Well, leave her here, maybe she'll change her mind or something and they taught her to clean and change bedpans and they were making a nurse out of her. And she was discovered to be pregnant, of course, and she was eventually obliged to go back to her husband. She never forgave him any of this. She never liked him. She had six children, and whatever he did, he would—they lived at the post Aunt Nell was born there you see—then he was sent to . . . and probably Mike (I don't know where Mike was born). But then they were up in Montana. What was the fort?*

Civil War: California, Benicia Barracks (1860)

The earliest official record of Michael is from his military records, 20 September **1860** where he enlisted at the Benicia Barracks, into the 6th U.S. Infantry, Company G for 5 years under Captain Boots. His enlistment described him as having gray eyes, sandy hair, fair complexion and standing 5 feet 6 inches. *Munnie* insisted that Michael was a Captain, even though so far, no record indicates this. This is also the first mention of Michael's middle name, *Romanus*.

> *Captain Michael Romanus Roche served with the North-South Civil War in the 7th Calvary regular army. He later served as an Indian Scout in the Indian Wars*

The 6th U.S. Infantry history started in California at the New San Diego Barracks until August 1860 and then at Benicia Barracks. On 21 October **1861**, the company departed by steamboat for Panama where they crossed the isthmus by rail and then by steamer to New York. They went on duty and was scattered around a number of locations ranging from San Francisco to encampments near the California-Oregon border. In April 1861, orders were received at the regiment's headquarters in San Francisco to concentrate these detachments in Washington, D.C. This order was compiled as quickly as possible but because of the distances involved and the insufficient shipping, the first detachment of the regiment did not reach Washington, D.C. until 31 October 1861. Other parts of the unit followed rapidly thereafter. On 31 January **1862**, the entire regiment had concentrated at Washington. Unofficial names of this unit were Levi C. Booten's Infantry; John McCleary's Infantry; Montgomery Bryant's Infantry and George W. Wallace's Infantry. From 19-20 February 1862, treated for Catarrhus.

VIRGINIA (1862)

5 April-4 May, Siege of Yorktown; 25 June-1 July, Seven Days Battle; 26 June, Battle, Mechanicsville, Beaver Dam Creek (Ellison's Mills); 27 June, Battle, Gaines Mill, Cold Harbor, Chickahominy; 27 June, Michael was reported as being wounded at Gaines Mills; 30 June, Engagement, Turkey Bridge (Melvern Cliff); 1 July, Battle, Malvern Hill, Crew's Farm (Poindexter's Farm); 28 August-2 September, Campaign, Northern Virginia (Second Bull Run Campaign); 29 August, Battle, Groveton; 30 August, Battle, Second Bull Run, Manassas (Groveton Heights).

MARYLAND (1862)

6-22 September, Maryland Campaign; 16-17 September, Battle, Antietam, Sharpsburg; 19 September, Action, Sharpsburg, Shepherdstown, Blackford's Ford (Boteler's Ford), Williamsport, Potomac River.

VIRGINIA (1862-1863)

20 September, Action, Shepherdstown Ford; 26 October-10 November, Operations, Loudon, Faquier and Rappahannock Counties; 3 November, Reconnaissance to Snicker's Gap and Skirmish; 11-16 December, wounded his hand, Battle, Fredericksburg, reported by Capt. Levi C. Brooks, 6 Reg., Co. G; 11-6 December, Michael is mentioned on a list of casualties before Fredericksburg where his hand is severely wounded and is reported as having a gunshot near the top of his head on the right side, in Michael's own handwriting:

> *A baynat cut in the chin at the Battle of Gainesville, VA 5 miles from city of Richmond VA the Rebel Capital then 2ndly at Fredericksburg, VA 14 Dec 1862. How I came to the mily hospital from the Battlefield*

in or neer the Rapanack River, Va by the cars from the Rappanak to Acqua Creek on he Potamack River from Acqua Creek to Washington DC by Steamboat thence to Mt. Pleasant Hospital Washington DC. I was treated by Dr. McCall, Hospital Surgeon at Mt. Pleasant Washington about 3 or 4 months after I came to the hospital I was examined by a bord of doctors a put into the 2nd Battaloon of the veteran researve care when I was about 8 (?) months.

20-24 January, Burnside's "Mud March"; 27 April-6 May, Chancellorsville Campaign; 1-5 May, Battle, Chancellorsville.

PENNSYLVANIA (1863)

11 June-24 July, Gettysburg Campaign; 1-3 July, Battle, Gettysburg; 5-24 July, Pursuit to near Manassas Gap, Virginia; July, Michael transferred to Company H.

NEW YORK (1863-1865)

16 August 1863-May 1865, he served in New York City. The Draft Riots had only recently appeared there and it was feared that similar disturbances would flare up once the draft was restarted. The regiment remained on duty in New York City, headquartered near City Hall for a brief period of time and then moved to Fort Hamilton, Brooklyn. The regiment remained here on garrison duty; 11-19 March, hospitalized for jaundice, Fort Columbus, New York Harbor; 26-27 April, hospitalized for Caterrhus, Fort Wood on Bedloe's Island in the harbor.

SOUTH CAROLINA (1865)

20 September, Michael was honorably discharged at Hilton Head, South Carolina. There is the first mention of him having a gunshot wound near the top of his head on the right side.

WASHINGTON, D.C. (1865)

Michael was treated at the Brigade and the Post Hospital on 14th Street at Carver and Mt. Pleasant Hospitals. Examination describes him as being 5 feet, 6 inches, of fair complexion with gray eyes.

IRELAND (1865?)

Roache descendants mention that Michael took a 6 month to a year's furlough in 1865 and went to Ireland to visit his family. Sammie interviewed her mother, Helen.

> (Helen) . . . *when he was thirty years old, he went, he had a year's furlough, or a long furlough of some kind, and he went home to Ireland, he had saved . . . his money and oh he was a credit to the twon and a great fellow. And she* [Margaret] *was a beautiful little fifteen year old, who had never had shoes on probably. And they got married. And they came . . .*

WASHINGTON, D.C. (1866-1869)

30 September, Michael re-enlisted for a second time for 3 years at Ordinance Detachment; 27 March 1867-2 April, treated for neuralgia; 8-10 October, treated for fever at Reynold's Barracks, 44 Reg., Co. H; (1868) 28-31 July treated for headache; 30 September discharged; 5 October, third re-enlistment for 3 years; (1869) 24 March transferred to Co. C; 17 May, transferred to Co. K; 21-22 March, treated for sprain; 20-21 April, treated for acute diarrhea.

INDIANA TERRITORY (1870-1871)

17-22 October 1870, treated for fever at hospital, Fort Sill, 6 Reg., Co. F; 21-22 November treated for fever; 23-29 November, treated for fever; 5-14 December, treated for acute bronchitis; 17-20 January 1871, treated for fever at Fort Gibson; 1-4 March, treated for acute bronchitis; 21-22 March, treated for sprain; 20-21 April, treated for acute diarrhea; 17-19 May, treated for inebriation; 21-26 June, treated for whitlow; 23-29 November, treated for fever; 5-14 December, treated for acute bronchitis.

DAKOTA TERRITORY (1871)

5 October, Michael discharged at Fort Rice.

FORT LEAVENWORTH, KANSAS (1872-1876)

28 November 1872, Michael re-enlisted for the last time for 5 years.

> (Helen) . . . *"Munnie" Roache-Mottin mentioned that Margaret apparently had no idea that Michael was in the military until they were married. This seemed frightful for her. He apparently had made her a promise as she commented, "I'd have my own carriage, you told me. You just bought me." When she got well (from what, I wander? Possibly when she was in the hospital in the first place?) she refused absolutely to go back to her husband, as she wasn't going to have any part of him. So the sisters at the hospital said, "We'll leave her here and maybe she'll change her mind or something." And so they taught her to clean and change bedpans and they were making a nurse out of her. She soon discovered that she was pregnant (with Nell) and eventually obliged to go back to her husband. She never forgave him for any of this, as she never like him. She commented, "I won't be a nurse and wash their filthy asses.*

1 December **1872**, Michael received a bill for a nurse uniform (provided by Leger Brosnahan) for which Margaret was to become a nurse via St. John's Hospital, Leavenworth; 18-19 March **1873**, Michael was treated for sprain at post hospital, 5 Reg., Co. A.; 1 September, Michael and Margaret Josephine Kanelly were married by Rev. John Schultz at the Immaculate Conception Church, Leavenworth with Thomas Malady and Johanna Schmit as witnesses; 3 September, she was hospitalized, it doesn't list why she was there or for how long; January **1874**, *Mary Ellen* could have been conceived as she was born on 3 October; 18 October, Mary Ellen baptized. *Munnie* mentioned that not long after Nell was born, about 6 months old, Margaret returned to Ireland with Nell for about a year and a half; May 1875, Michael was transferred to Co. E.; May 1876, Michael was transferred to Co. I.; Before November, Margaret may have returned, as their next son, *Michael*, may have been conceived, as on 9 August he was born; 12 August, Michael was baptized.

Montana: Fort Keogh (1877-1883)

The Roache family was found living here in a few sources. According to, Hoopes, Lorman L. (year?) *This Last West: Miles City, Montana Territory, and Environs, 1876-1886 The People, The Geography, The Incredible History* . . . , which is a compilation of newspapers Hoopes put together of that town. This and a census mentioned the family. **1877**, 28 November, Michael was honorably discharged at Tongue River Barracks, Fort Keogh; Michael and Margaret were proven as *First Families of Montana* (4 February 2003 by R.S. Baskas) as they had settled into Montana, before it became a state, on 8 November 1889. Michael took up land on section 10 on Tongue River, 3 miles south of Miles City; Later on, Margaret rejoined her husband with their children, Nell and Michael Jr.; **1878**, 29 December, their third child, *Katherine Margaret*, was born on their parent's ranch near Miles City. **1879**, 22 June, Katherine was baptized at St. Mary's Church, Bismarck, North Dakota. Roache descendants mentioned that *Jim Connely* was living in Leavenworth when he was sent to Montana in 1879 to work on the Roache family ranch while Michael was working at the post. An **1880** Census, Miles City, Custer County, Montana shows Michael, Margaret and their children, Mary Ellen, Michael and Catherine living there; 3 October 1880, their fourth child, *John Joseph*, was born on parent's ranch near Miles City and on 31 October, he was baptized at a catholic church in Miles City. Sammie continues her interview with Helen:

> (Helen) . . . *Battles with the Indians continued until 1881 when Sitting Bull surrendered at Fort Buford and the Indians were confined to reservations. Indian women worked as nursemaids for the few officers' wives who lived inside the fort. Frequently Indian men came to the fort on business and were not as colorful as today's movie Indians. Wagons-loaded with supplies and drawn by several pairs of mules-rumbled in and out of the fort at long intervals. "Munnie" recalls deep mud and intense cold, tall windblown grass, swimming in a little stream at the foot of the hill. Mike and Nell, her brother and sister, spent long summer days playing in the cool water of the stream. One afternoon as a supply wagon came down the road to cross the little bridge that spanned the water, the two older children plunged unto the shallows off the seat of an abandoned wagon from which they had been diving.*

Kate sat watching the wagon. As it neared, the driver lifted his long bullwhip and sent it flying toward her. Its length coiled ever so gently around her tiny naked body and just as quickly unwound and returned to the air beyond the threesome. Her older siblings splashed up to examine Kate's pink skin but found no mark to confirm the adventure . . . And Mother at that age must have been three or four years old, since she remembers them pulling her out of the creek by her long hair.

14 March **1882**, their fifth child, **Daniel O'Connell**, was born on their parent's ranch near Miles City; 2-12 March, Michael (5th Reg, Co. K) was treated for acute diarrhea; 27 March-1 May, treated for fever; 24 September, Daniel was baptized at his parent's ranch near Miles City; 6 November, he began filling for a pension in Miles City; Family mentions that some of the Indians from the area helped babysit their kids. Rev. E. W. Lindesmith was the chaplain at the Fort from 1881-9. He performed mass at numerous homes in town, one being Michael and Margaret's! According to my Aunt Eileen Becker, Margaret rode her covered wagon from Montana to Leavenworth alongside Plumb Creek as she came into Kickapoo, Kansas. On her travels, she had stopped to spend the night on the trail. One night she awoke to the moaning of an Indian that had slept next to her wagon. When she woke the next day, she found a turkey by her wagon. Apparently this was a gift from the Indian for letting him sleep next to her wagon.

KANSAS: FORT LEAVENWORTH (1884-PRESENT)

16 January **1884**, their sixth and seventh children, which were twins, **William "Bert" Patrick** and **James** were born. At this time, the family lived at 523 Cheyenne until Michael retired; 27 January, the twins were baptized at the Immaculate Conception Church witnessed by *James Connely*. James, the new born, was discovered by me some years later by accident while researching baptismal records at St. Joseph's. I found that Bert's birth date, baptismal date and parents matched James'. This was the only place James was found; 26 June, James, the twin, was the first to die in the family. Because the family had no plot at that time, Mt. Calvary Cemetery explained that the baby was buried on the hill with the other infants and with a brick for a headstone. His stone hasn't been located yet. Margaret was successfully proven as a *PIONEER OF*

KANSAS (by R. S. Baskas) which was submitted for publication in THE FORGOTTEN SETTLERS OF KANSAS, Volume 24, by the Kansas Council of Genealogical Societies, Inc., 2001. Kate described her parents' clothing as she remembers them:

> *Mama's idea of elegance was a black sateen dress, not satin, sateen. It was very fine and she wore it only on special occasions. She wore a big bustle in back which was the fashion and a big white apron. Even when she went to visit she wore the big white apron. My father, when he got out of the army, bought a suit. He called it pepper and salt and I remember it was a grey, sort of black and white speckles. My mother thought it was ugly. I remember she laughed at it and it made my father angry. I thought it was beautiful.*

1885 Leavenworth County, Kansas Census shows Michael, Margaret Mary Ellen (10 years old), Michael, Kate, John, Daniel and Willy in the household. **1887**, 23 March, Margaret Josephine Kanelly-Roache was naturalized. **1889**, 19 January, eighth child, *Joseph M.*, was born. Apparently Joseph had a middle initial, M., which is only known in directories; 10 March, Joseph M. was baptized sometime after his retirement,

> (Helen) . . . *her father went out on some kind of mission. And he must have been in the army, and be killed on this, but not a war. Like they were building bridges out on maneuvers.*

Michael had written Margaret explaining about his job. He worked as a contractor in the swamp clearing where he soon died of a chill and was apparently buried in Louisiana. According to an affidavit in his military records, he died on **1891**, 10 January, on Dallas Plantation, Madison Parish, Louisiana; His headstone has yet to be found. When Margaret filed for a pension in Leavenworth, she mentioned having received the affidavit on the death. After this, Margaret then started living at 611 Cheyenne until she met and married Daniel Richard Pike. According to *Munnie*, apparently Daniel had met Michael before he gave Daniel a promise, "OK Dan, you can have her after my death." Their first child to move out was Kate as she lived at 617 Pawnee.

Margaret Josephine Kanelly (M1) Michael Roache

Mary Ellen "Nell" Roache m. Patrick Leo Cantwell
Michael Bernard Roache m. Katherine Francis Cotter
Catherine Margaret "Munnie" Roache m. Leger Nicholas Mottin Jr.
John Joseph Roache
Daniel O'Connell Roache m. Elizabeth Lynch
William Patrick "Bert" Roache (twin) m. Margaret Dykstra
James Roache (twin)
Joseph M. Roache

CHAPTER IV

PIKE

Researcher
Richard S. Baskas

Contributors
Margaret K. "M.K." Baskas and (Dr.) Leger Brosnahan

QUEEN'S COUNTY, IRELAND

According to his obituary and headstone, Daniel Richard Pike was born on 16 March **1852** in Queen's County, Ireland. Kansas census shows him immigrating about **1872** and naturalized in **1876**. Baskas family members mentioned him coming to America with a *Dutch Nolan* via Missouri/ Wyandotte County, Kansas. Kansas directories show him being in Leavenworth by **1885**.

LEAVENWORTH, KANSAS (1885-1888)

Leavenworth directories show him at various addresses which were on Shawnee, possibly while working for the street department: **1885**—lived at 202 Shawnee; **1886**—lived at 208 north 5th upstairs; **1887**—he's not listed; **1888**—he's a foreman city grading living at 621 Shawnee.

BLAINE, KANSAS (1890-1891)

According to family papers, *Munnie* mentioned that Daniel was a big wig in the Masonry. The Masonic Lodge in Leavenworth directed me to contact what ended up being Topeka, Kansas. Within a few minutes of providing a few details and waiting—Daniel was initiated on 17 June **1890**, passed the tests on 13 December **1890** and was raised to the 3rd degree on 10 January **1891**. This took place at lodge #337, Frederick Lodge, Blaine, Kansas. Becoming a Freemason, there are three degrees of Craft or Blue Lodge Freemasonry: *Entered Apprentice*, degree of an Initiate, making one a Freemason; *Fellow Craft*, intermediate degree, involved in learning; and *Master Mason*, "third degree", a necessity for participation in most aspects of Masonry. According to **United Grand Lodge of England [1815]** (2005). "Aims and Relationships of the Craft", General requirements to be a regular Freemason: Be a man who comes of his own free will; Believe in Supreme Being (The form of which is left to open interpretation by the candidate); Be at least the minimum age (18-25 years old depending on the jurisdiction); Be of good morals, and of good reputation; Be of sound mind and body (Lodges had in the past denied membership because of a physical disability, however, now, if a potential candidate says a disability will not cause problems, it will not be held against him); Be free-born (or "born free", i.e. not born a slave or bondsman); Have character references, as well as one or two references from current Masons, depending on jurisdiction.

LEAVENWORTH, KANSAS (1891)

Leavenworth directories show him boarding at a French Hotel, 203-205 Shawnee.

KANSAS CITY, KANSAS (1892-1894)

On 22 February **1892**, Pike married Margaret Josephine Kanelly-Roache in Kansas City, Kansas, performed by George Monahan, a probate judge. Daniel was listed as being 39 years old and Margaret, at 35. Daniel worked in a roundhouse near fifth and Ann Street for a few years. 19 February **1893**, their first child, *Thomas*, was born; 23 April, John Roache died by accident and was buried somewhere in Kansas City. Pike family lived in a section house foot of Garfield Avenue then later to Ann Avenue; 22 April **1894**, their second child, *Charles*, was born.

LEAVENWORTH, KANSAS (1894-1896?)

Daniel worked as a foreman living on the westside of 4th between Elizabeth and Isabel. On 9 January **1895**, Nell Roache (then 20 years old) married Patrick Cantwell at Sacred Heart, Leavenworth.

KANSAS CITY, MISSOURI

The Pike household moved to what was then Heim's Brewery. He worked for the Missouri Pacific Railroad, which supposedly ran through Tipton during the Civil War. His family was to have attended the German Church.

LEAVENWORTH, KANSAS (1895 TO PRESENT)

The **1895** Leavenworth census shows Daniel, Margaret and their children living at 712 2nd Street (Michael Roache, Kate Roache, Daniel Roache, Willy Roache, Joseph Roache, Thomas Pike, Charles Pike, Patrick and Nellie Roache-Cantwell (appeared to have moved in with her parents), (Robert Pike wasn't listed so wasn't born yet). James and Kate (Margaret Pike's sister) Barry seemed to have lived next door or down the street with their children, Mary Ellen, Kate, Agnes, Margaret, and James; 25 November, *Robert* was born. By this same time, Kate Roache moved to 617 Pawnee while she worked at Fort Leavenworth. **1896**, 5 January, Robert Pike was baptized. Michael Bernard and Katie Roache shared a place at 609 N. 8th, Katie was still working at the fort. **1897**, 23 November, *Leo Pike* was born and his parents were living at 816 Shawnee. **1899**, 31 December, the Pike's had their last child, *Margaret*, while they were living at 617 Pawnee. Strangely enough, it's been said that her birthday is 1 January 1900 since she was born so close to this date. I found 2 pieces of evidence to suggest 1899, her birth record and Kansas census. **1900** Kansas census shows the Pike's lived at 617 Pawnee with all their children including Daniel, William and Joseph Roache; 28 November, Kate Roache married Leger Mottin. The same census showed the Cantwell's, Nell and Patrick, their daughter Margaret K. rented 1207 2nd Street while Patrick was a car inspector. **1901**, Michael Bernard Roache lived at 617 Pawnee and later married Katherine Cotter. **1902-1904** Bert Roache lived at 307 Lawrence. **1909** Joseph Roache moved to 216 Pawnee. **1917**, Bert married Margaret Dykstra, but divorced by 1920; 3 March, Anna Eileen Becker was born; 8 September, Robert Pike and Mamie Bodenschatz were married; Leo and

Chet Pike entered World War I. **1918**, Thomas and Robert Pike entered military; Daniel Pike retired. **1919**, 20 May, Lillian Mae Becker was born; 1 December, Daniel and Margaret bought 400 Pawnee from Mary Larkin for $1000.00. At the time they bought the house, there was no kitchen and so (according to family) Daniel later added this himself. In the later years, their children worked in the coalmines in southern Leavenworth. Daniel was a member of what was then the A.O.U.W. (Ancient Order of Union Workers). Its name was changed to Leavenworth Legion Select Knights in 1888. It appeared that Daniel never used any banking business. In their master bedroom Daniel made a hole in the floorboard so to stash all their money and then covered it with a piece of carpet or linoleum. This was also used by his future son-in-law, John Baskas, when they later lived there.

> (Helen) . . . *He was a ratty (?) bandy legged little Irishman who never did more than work in the freight yards or something and or the mine. He used to come home black and carrying . . . he worked with a light on his head.*

This may explain why I heard stories of him using a cane. Margaret was a member of the American Gold Star War Mothers, Inc. This group consisted of mothers who had lost a son or daughter in a war and therefore were given a gold star. None of Daniel and Margaret's children was killed during any war, even though their sons did serve in World War I and/or II. In **1920**, Pike household lived at 521 Cheyenne, Daniel and Margaret, their children Thomas, Charles, step-son William Roache, daughter and son-in-law John and Margaret Pike-Becker and their two daughters Eileen and Lilly Mae, and their other son and daughter-in-law living at 530 Cheyenne, Robert and Mammie Pike (next door?); **1922**, Thomas Pike moved to 711 Metropolitan; **1923**, 24 January, Daniel and Margaret sold their house to John and Margaret Baskas as they moved to 522 Cheyenne. **1930**, Chet lived with his parents as he was married, but his wife and kids aren't mentioned. **1933**, 27 December, Margaret Josephine Pike died at her daughter's house at 400 Pawnee and was buried at Mt. Calvary. **1933**, Michael Bernard Roache, Margaret's son, was supposed to be living in Hardin, Montana. **1935**, 24 May, Daniel Pike died at the Baskas farm in Kickapoo; buried at Mt. Calvary.

> (Helen) . . . *they had some of the most beautiful little walnut tables and chairs and things there. I was just crazy for them,*

and when Grandmother died, Mother [Munnie] *wouldn't even let me ask for them.*

Margaret Josephine Kanelly (M2) Daniel Richard Pike

Thomas Cleveland Pike m. Zell Spain
Charles Francis Pike m1. Raymonde Lorre/Loure, m2. Jane Manning
Robert Emmet Pike m. Mamie Katherine Bodenschatz
Leo Clement Pike m. Frances Mary Heckman
Margaret Pike m1. John William Becker, m2. John Burke Baskas, nm.
Jerome "Jerry" Harrison Wolf

CHAPTER V

BARRY

Researcher
Richard S. Baskas

The only sources of information that has been able to be reliable are from Mt. Calvary cemetery, obituaries, census and the Kansas Room at the Leavenworth Public Library. An **1884** Kansas census has *Kate Keanneally* immigrated to the states (making her about 17 years old). Strangely enough, it seems that she wasn't born until Margaret went back to Ireland and found out she had another sibling? **1886**, February, *Mary Ellen Barry*, was born. **1887**, 4 December, *Catherine "Kate" Barry*, was born while her parents lived at 608 North 4th Street. **1890**, Mary is only seen in 1890 Kansas census. Kate married James Henry Barry Sr., no record has been researched. James Sr. worked on various railway companies and at the Abernathy Furniture Company in Leavenworth; member of the Brotherhood of American Yeoman. Only the 1905 Kansas census shows an *Aggie Barry* (male) b.; **1892**, 2 February, *Brigit Agnes Barry* was born; 10 July, *Margaret Elizabeth Barry* was born; **1894**, 18 September, *James Henry Barry Jr.* was born; **1895**, Leavenworth census shows Daniel and Margaret Pike's family living at 712 2nd Street—Michael Roache, Kate Roache, Daniel Roache, Willy Roache, Joseph Roache, Thomas Pike, Charles Pike, Patrick and Nellie (Roache) Cantwell moved in once they were married, (Robert Pike not born yet), James and Kate (Margaret Pike's sister) Barry (next door?) later Barry Tavern (?) lived next door with their family, Mary Ellen,

Kate, Agnes, Margaret, and James. **1929**, 28 November, Kate died at her granddaughter's home, Mrs. Ruth West, of 33 North Tremont, Kansas City, Kansas; 13 December, James purchased burial plots at Mount Calvary at section 2, block 6. **1932**, 27 March, James died in Leavenworth at his son's residence of 110 Isabelle Street. Both buried Mt. Calvary, just a row from her sister's plot, Margaret Pike-Roache.

Mary Ellen Barry
Catherine Barry m. Morris/Maurice Aliff
Brigit Agnes Barry m. William Jerome Snyder
Mary/Margaret Elizabeth Barry m. Henry Pickering
James Henry Barry m. Florence Belle Hamblin

CHAPTER VI

GENERATION 1

Researcher
Richard S. Baskas

Contributors
James "Jim" A. Baskas, John "Buddy" Baskas;
Margaret K. "M.K." Baskas and (Dr.) Leger Brosnahan

JOSEPH BASKAS *AND*
JOHANNA MCMAHON

FRANK JOSEPH BASKAS, b. 8 November 1863, Kickapoo, Kansas; bapt. 16 November 1863, IMAC; coal miner and policeman for nearly 18 years; m. Annie Marie Killilay 17 November 1894; Annie, b. 11 December 1867, d. 23 May 1909 of TB; d. 4 December 1911 Leavenworth; both buried at Mt. Calvary. (unknown where he's buried; she has 2 stones; have both obituaries).

i.   *Marie Baskas* m. Clarence John DeWoody
ii. *Francis Joseph Baskas*
iii. *Thomas Joseph Baskas* m1. Mickey, m2. Mary Ruth Pistorius
iv. *Walter William Baskas* m. Lois Darlene Hubbard
v.   *Anna Josephine Baskas*
vi. *James "Jimmy" Baskas (Fitzgerald)*

MARY C. BASKAS, b. 19 August 1865, Kickapoo, Kansas; bapt. 20 August 1865, IMAC; d. 23 May

1892, Leavenworth of heart disease; buried at Mt. Calvary (have stone).

ANTHONY BASKAS, b. 12 November 1867, Kickapoo, Kansas; bapt. 17 May 1868, IMAC; worked as a policeman; his name is seen as *Abe* by his wife, Ella, only in his will; Ella b. 22 November 1869 St. Joseph, Missouri, d. 30 December 1916 Leavenworth, apparently had children from a previous marriage, initially buried in a single plot in Mt. Muncie but was moved next to her daughter, Bertie; d. 5 December 1916 Leavenworth of Bright's Disease. (buried?)

JOSEPH "WINDY" BASKAS JR., b. 16 March 1869, Kickapoo, Kansas; bapt. 18 April 1869, IMAC; worked as a coal miner and train station terminal bridge while living on North 5th Street; d. 24 February 1944, Leavenworth (have obituary, need stone).

JENNIE/JANE BASKAS, b. 7 February 1871, Kickapoo, Kansas; bapt. 13 May 1871, IMAC; lived at 228 Ottawa in 1890 and worked as a waiter at Continental Hotel in 1892-3; adopted by Genevieve Glynn once her mother died; m. John Perry and lived in Kansas City, Missouri; he retired from municipal engineering department, Kansas City, Missouri for many years; he d. 21 July 1941 Leavenworth, buried

Mt. Calvary; was to be at St. Joe's mental hospital; d. 4 January 1943 (need obituary, stone and burial).

JAMES BASKAS, b. 1872, Kickapoo, Kansas (listed only in 1885 Kansas census); family mentions he may have lived on a farm and/or may have been adopted.

ELIZABETH BASKAS, b. 30 August 1874, Kickapoo, Kansas; bapt. 13 October 1876, IMAC; m. Michael F. Glynn, 11 January 1899, Leavenworth (Michael b. November 1864 Iowa, of Irish immigrants, Lawrence and Helen M.); Kansas 1900 census showed one of their children had died but no name; 1901-4, laborer at Pittsburg VP and BB Co. while living at 570 2nd Ave.; 1905-12 miner for Carr Coal Mining and Mfg. Co. while living at 1209 S. 2nd St.; 1913-15, he lived in Walsenburg, Colorado; 1915-23 living at 1209 S. 2nd St.; Kansas 1920 census, Michael's mother lived with him; d. 3 February/2 March 1923, Leavenworth; buried at Mt. Calvary. (have her obituary, need stone); d. 18 December 1914.

i.   *Elizabeth Glynn*
ii. *Helen Glynn* m. George Meeker
iii. *Blanche Glynn* m. John D. Becher
iv. *Joseph Lawrence Glynn* Sr. m1. Barbara J.; m2. Alice L. "Cy" Glynn

v.   *John Walter Glynn* m. Dorothy Alice Martin

vi. *Genevieve Glynn* m. Leo W. Burns

WILLIAM BASKAS, b. 20 December 1875, Kickapoo, Kansas; bapt. 13 October 1876 IMAC; grocer at 6th and Pawnee Street; bootlegged behind his store; member of the A.O.U.W. Lodge #122; never married; [There is a William Baskas, b. 26 November 1877 (date on stone) Kansas; lived 1209 S. 2nd St.; registered (serial #2053) for World War I when 41 years of age (at 1918) and coal miner at time; listed nearest relative as John Baskas of same address; employed at RICK_UTSON (name on card was unclear) and John Glynn was his supervisor.] d. 8 September 1935 Kansas; buried at Mt. Calvary (have stone).

J. W. (JOSEPH WILLIAM?) BASKAS, b. 1880, Kickapoo, Kansas; m. Violet McNeil on 18 July 1904 in Leavenworth (no records at Sacred Heart or IMAC); (need stone and burial)

i.   *Clarence Joseph Baskas*

KATHERINE BASKAS, b. 21 September 1881, Kickapoo, Kansas; (relative's obituaries of these dates mention her being in these areas) Kansas City in 1902; Chicago, Illinois in 1935 and Los Angeles, California in 1944; d. January 1973 Los Angeles, California (Kathryn Backus, SS# 554-12-7628, last 90024); (need obituary, stone or burial).

JOHN BURKE BASKAS, b. 27 September 1882, Kickapoo, Kansas; bapt. 29 October 1882, Sacred Heart Church, Kickapoo with John McMahon and Catherine Mahoney as sponsors; lived with sister Elizabeth Glynn in 1905; worked in the Carr coal mine in the 1920s; m. Margaret Pike, 11 April **1921**, in court in Jackson County, Missouri.

When was the Kickapoo farm bought and who lived here first? Who bought he Lowemont farm? Did lived at the Kickapoo farm?; 17 December, "Buddy" was born, at the Kickapoo farm?

On 24 January **1923**, John and Margaret bought the 400 Pawnee house from Margaret's mother. The rest of their children were born here, starting in 1924. All their children attended the Cathedral Grade School and IMAC. Most of them joined the military before finishing school or soon after and therefore moved out on their own.

Family mentions that the house was once a halfway station or stagecoach built before the Civil War. It had a cellar where the soldiers would store their ammo. Visitors would stop for the night and visit the bar. Some people that once visited the house were Canadian Mounties and Elliot Ness, who was the FBI, The Untouchables. My aunt Eileen (Margaret's daughter) once sat on Elliot's lap at the bar. The main business that John had, which was at the house, was running his own bar. Up until the Prohibition of the 1920s, liquor was legal in the town. But when it became illegal, tough times began for John. John then began finding ways of supplying liquor for his bar business. He was said to have his own distillery in the cellar. As a child, my father remembers hear popping noises from the cellar as the tops of the bottles popped when the yeast fermented. The house seemed to hold more hiding spaces than one could remember. My father would roam the house care free and accidentally find some of these hidden spaces where John had stashed away a lot of his homemade liquor. My father would obviously get yelled at by his mother to get away from there.

The only place that was legal for liquor was Missouri. And so John would make many trips across the Fort Leavenworth Bridge to Missouri. This bridge was the only access close enough for him, besides the terminal bridge where he would most certainly get caught. Family mentions that he would get caught constantly once he came back in

via the fort and was pulled over once he reached Metropolitan and 7th Street. If he had been arrested, his bar business would have been no more and so instead he was given tickets. The original building, where he bought his liquor, is still there, down the street in Missouri right off the bridge, but is now a gas station and quick shop.

The Pawnee house had no original stairs going to the cellar, just "swing" chain stairs. During some of the tornadoes, the family and whoever was at the bar, all went downstairs using the "stairs". After this went on for some time, this one guy got tired of it and decided to build it. The straw that broke the camel's back was when Margaret's daughter, Lilly Mae, hurt herself using the stairs and so "real" stairs were finally put in.

The house also had a few barns in the backyard. When the circus was in town, some of the circus people offered the family tickets in exchange to put their advertisements on the barn walls.

John was a member of the Fraternal Order of Eagles Aerie No. 55. On 4 January 1934, John bought a cemetery plot at Mt. Calvary on Lot 60, Block 8, Section 2. He died at St. John's Hospital in Leavenworth on 9 January 1954 and was buried at Mt. Calvary.

Margaret continued living in the Pawnee house until about 1962.

Her son, Michael, kept the bar business as *Mike's Place* in 1966 and later was run under his brother and sister-in-law, Pat and Dorothy from 1968-77. By 1962, Margaret moved to 7th Street. Sometime later, the city bought the Pawnee house and had it torn down. Most of Margaret's children served in World War II—Marines, Army or Navy. Her first two children, her daughters, didn't serve. Her other daughter, Margaret Katherine "MK", was the only daughter to serve, which was the Navy's WAVES. My father and another uncle were the only two boys who didn't serve. One time, Margaret had typed a letter for her daughter, M.K., who was in the Navy serving at Pearl Harbor, Hawaii at the time. The strange thing was that M.K. received the letter two weeks after it was mailed, but she couldn't read it. The problem was that the plane that had delivered it had crashed in the ocean. She couldn't read it since the ink was handwritten and was so badly blurred, but the address was typed and was legible.

Margaret later moved to 700 Osage where she lived for some years. While her children served, Margaret was involved in many military organizations, the V.F.W. Auxiliary, American Legion Auxiliary and the American War Mothers as well as many other organizations. From 1969 to 1970, she was the Vice President of the Fraternal Order of Eagles Aerie No. 55. She was also madam President in 1970 and then Junior Past President from 1971-2. On 16 December 1957, The Leavenworth Times had recognized her as possibly having one of the largest "service" families in Leavenworth since seven of her 12 living children had served in various military branches. In 1974, she retired. On 30 December 1979, all her children and extended family threw her a surprise 80th birthday party in Leavenworth at the Fort's Officer's Club. On 3 April 1985, she died in Lansing, Kansas and was buried next to her husband.

i. *John Joseph "Buddy" Baskas* m. Mary Margaret Crook

ii. *Leo Daniel "Blackie" Baskas* m. Mildred Overman/Eubanks

iii. *Francis William "Frank" Baskas* m. Louetta Katherine Kenny

iv. *Thomas Emmett "Tom" Baskas* m. Wilda June Snider

v. *Patrick Jerome "Pat" Baskas* m. Dorothy Mae Petit

vi. *Robert Edward "Bobby" Baskas* m. Vivian "Tudy" Rose Heitlinger

vii. *Margaret Katherine "M.K." Baskas*

viii. *Ralph Vincent "Porky" Baskas* m1. Catherine Martin; m2. JoAnn Shasick

ix. *Johanna Marie Baskas*

x. *Michael Charles "Mike" Baskas* m. Una Mae Shasick

xi. *James Anthony "Jimmy" Baskas* m1. Betty Emma Karnes; m2. Marianne Lane; m3. Virginia Heintzelman

ROSE BASKAS, (062-16-0397), b. 22 August 1892, Kansas; 1935, Kansas City, Missouri as Rose Kearney (lived near sister, Mrs. John Perry?); 27 August 1957 12 Hinsdale St, Brooklyn, New York?; d. November 1973; Records show that the last place of her was in New Rochelle, Westchester, New York, 10801; (need obituary, stone and burial)

MARGARET JOSEPHINE KENALLY AND MICHAEL ROACHE

MARY ELLEN **"NELL"** ROACHE, b. 3 October 1874, Ft. Leavenworth, Kansas; bapt. 18 October 1874, IMAC by James O'Reilly, Michael McLaughlin and Mary Cronin were godparents; On 9 January 1895, Nell and Patrick Leo Cantwell were married, Sacred Heart, Leavenworth, Katherine Roach (her sister?) and James Fitzgerald as witnesses; 1895 Leavenworth census showed them living with the Pike's; apparently Edward and Margaret K. were born here before the Cantwell's were to move in 1900 at 1207 2nd Street and apparently the rest of their children

were born there. Patrick worked as a car inspector on the railroad and had contracted TB. El Paso, Texas was the best place to have it treated and so this is how their family ended up there. He was a member of the A.O.H. and W.O.W. He died on 28 December 1918 at 404 W. Overland Street in El Paso, Texas and was buried at Concordia Cemetery; Nell may have died in 12 December 1955, El Paso, Texas.

i. *Edward Patrick Cantwell*

ii. *Margaret Katherine Cantwell* m. Charles Joseph Arnold

iii. *Patrick Leo Cantwell* m. Margaret Hennessey

iv. *Vincent Bernard Cantwell* m. Lillian Arron

v. *Francis Joseph Cantwell* m. Madeline Seibert

vi. *Mary Geraldine Cantwell* m1. Leonard Wilson Brown; m2. Robert L. Flynn

vii. *John Lillis Cantwell* m. Mary Virginia Cowles

viii. *Robert Emmet Sydney Cantwell*

MICHAEL **BERNARD** ROACHE, (#516038577), b. 9 August 1877, Ft. Leavenworth, Kansas; bapt. 12 August 1877, IMAC by Rev. J. O'Reilly; In 1896-7, lived with his sister, Katie, at 609 N. 8th Street. From 1899-1901, lived with Daniel and Catherine on 617 Pawnee; m. Katherine Francis Cotter on

Thanksgiving Day, November 1901 at IMAC with Frank Mottin and Minnie Cotter as witnesses. Family mentions that he helped resurface the road on Pawnee Street in front of 400 Pawnee; both lived as renters in 1930, Silver Bow County, Butte, Montana; 1930-5 as a minor in copper mines; in Billings, Montana in 1949; lived at 422 W. Pine Street for 4 years when he died at the Orange County hospital of a stroke on 23 April 1951 in Santa Ana, California. Funeral services were held at Smith and Tuthill; buried at Fairhaven cemetery Lawn AL, lot 155, space 1. Records don't exist since the area was just a cemetery.

KATHERINE MARGARET "MUNNIE" ROACHE, b. around midnight on 31 December 1879 inside the stockade wall of Fort Keogh, Miles City, Montana; bapt. 22 June 1879 by Rev. Chrysostou Toffa, St. Mary's Church, Bismarck, North Dakota with George Gerlach and Caroline Keogh (Keogh is just a coincidence) as witnesses. The Fort no longer exists but was one of the several military outposts established throughout the territory to protect the settlers and subdue the Indians. When Kate was 5 years old, her father was transferred from Fort Keogh to Fort Leavenworth, Kansas where the family lived at 5th and Cheyenne. She was interviewed by her granddaughter, Sammie, who wrote a folklore paper for a class regarding her grandmother's life during the Pioneering days (taken verbatim from her paper). School was a necessary evil, more to be endured than enjoyed. Children sat two to a desk. Usually the room was too hot or too cold, seldom comfortable. The best part of the day was recess. At some time the wall came down or was circumvented because she remembers playing games.

My father [Michael Sr.] was a devout Catholic and the only place I could go to school was to the sisters-I HATED it. At first it was just a girl's school and then they built another building 'cattacorner' from it and it was for boys and girls mixed. And the sister made the boys play in their yard and the girls had to go on beyond to their yard and there was a six foot fence between the two yards.

Kate remembered a happy memory centered around a happy adventure in eating:

Mother took a little tin bucket and me and we went out on the reservation [her mother thinks it's an Indian reservation but morel likely the Fort reservation] and gathered mushrooms. Every other day there'd be a 'plack' where you could get mushrooms and mama knew a mushroom from a toadstool. We used to get the little button mushrooms-mother'd get a bucketful-then we'd take them home and she'd turn one upside down and put a little salt on it and cook it on top of the range. We'd eat it and we loved it. They never tasted later like those we get on the reservation. These were the grandest tasting things I ever ate.

Regarding medicine and doctors:

I never remember seeing a doctor except when a baby came. When mother had a baby the doctor would come to the house and take the baby. We never were around when a baby was born. We were sent off, never left around. Lots of times there was no doctor, just some old woman took the baby.

When I was a girl there was a small pox scare along and I remember a smallpox vaccination would not take on me. All the school kids had to be vaccinated so I was. I was always bumping into someone who had his arm in a sling or was sore and tied up. You couldn't touch anybody that'd been vaccinated but my vaccination stayed put and I think I had to have it done over. Several years later I discover there was something on my shoulder back there that I thought was my vaccination breaking out all

through me. I still have the scar on my back.

My mother used to tie an old sock around our throat for sore throat-pin it and leave it there until the throat was well. Oh, it should be a sock that had been worn. I don't know if it was the heat in it or what but it wasn't a fresh-washed sock. She never put anything on it that I recall, just pinned the sock around the throat and left it there.

When asked if goose grease, a commonly used medicant, was ever put on the sock, she denied it but explained its use:

We always had geese. We kept geese. Everyone had geese. We at one at Christmas and saved the fat. We 'rended' it out and kept it. The goose geese got scarce and you went to the drugstore and bought a tablespoon for a quarter. As I recall they rubbed it on us if we had measles or a bad cold or put on our backs for pneumonia.

Regarding bad cuts or other wounds:

Once I had a very bad cut on my arm, just a very bad cut and mother took a little sugar and sprinkled it on there and spread turpentine on it. I thought the turpentine was worse than the cut but she said it would never be sour and it never was and that was the awfulest cut you ever saw. I think it's supposed to not leave as bad a scar, too. I remember mother looking around for a cobweb to put on one of the boy's cuts. I never knew why and never asked. She never put one on me.

Every fall with start of school, children were fitted out with their winter protection, an asafoedita bag, or "assaffidity" bag as there were commonly called:

You had to buy it at the drug store. Our mothers sewed it up in little bags and we had to wear it around our necks down inside our clothes. No decent person would let close to us. It smelled awful and was supposed to keep smallpox or something away. All children had o wear one but I don't remember adults wearing them. Looking back I don't know how the teachers stood it!

For measles mother kept us warm. We just had to die with heat and sweat it out. I don't think they gave any medicine for measles. I do remember having goose grease rubbed over my chest and covered with cloths but I'm not sure it was for measles. I think it was.

Easter called for unusual rituals, both religious and hygienic:

Easter was a big time always. There was Easter Water and the blessing of the big Easter candle in the church. Everybody got Easter Water to take home and blast the house and rooms. In a bad storm, they'd get the holy water out and sprinkle it around. People really kept Lent in those days. It was much harder than now. We always went to get ashes on our foreheads on Ash Wednesday. We had to. The nuns took us. There was a lot of praying, going to mass and to communion. We couldn't eat meat on Wednesdays or Fridays and no more than once a day other days. We are less than usual al the way around. Most of the good pious old women observed Lent closely. I don't know about the men. We didn't have any pious men to speak of.

Easter egg rolls we used to have only they were private affairs. Somebody would give a party and there'd be a lot of kids all bringing their own eggs. Then they'd mix them and hide them and the kids tried to find them. What you found were yours to keep. Eggs were only ten cents a dozen and we could eat all we wanted and then we'd brag about how many we'd eaten-lies mostly.

We used to color eggs with calico. We didn't have egg coloring like we do today. We covered an egg with pieces of cheap calico and sometimes the pattern of the material came off on the egg, sometimes it didn't. We'd sew it up tight and dunk it in the boiling water and leave it to boil. Sometimes the pattern came off beautifully. We'd use bluing, too, but we wee never allowed to eat those eggs for fear it might be poisoned from the dye. There eggs that we got good calico prints on we'd keep 'till they rotted.

Hair was washed infrequently in those days. Kate recalls that they always washed their hair on Good Friday, in preparation for Easter:

Nell and I had beautiful hair. Nell's was in a braid all the way down her back. Mine was not so long. The only time I remember washing my hair was at Easter and we had to wash it in the rain barrel beside the house. It was full of those little minnies [probably tadpoles], you know. We dipped in the wash our hair and again to rinse it but we didn't do much of either really. Then we sat in the sun like this (hair flipped forward over face) until it dried. Mama always kept the little ends of our braids clipped. I don't know why-whether it was a superstition or not but every first Friday she'd clip off the tip ends of our braids. She never forgot to do it [Catholics used to observe first Fridays of the month. Kate's mother was Irish-born and

this may have been a superstition in Ireland].

Regarding customs and pranks at Halloween:

On Halloween people locked their little ones up early but there'd be all kinds of pranks. I remember one time there was a nice home up the hill above us and some boys in town pushed this old wagon-or skeleton of a wagon it was-downhill and it rested across the railroad tracks and the train came along and got it.

One Halloween somebody took a whole little house that belonged to a man whose two daughters kept house for him-just took the whole house and moved it. Oh, yes, they used to do bad things, really bad things. They were the young men in town, not the boys. The girls never went out on Halloween.

Halloween parties were usually given by mothers for the girls and younger children. They'd fill a wash tub with water and the kids would kneel down around it and try to bit into apples floating in the water-without using hands. I never could. I don't believe anyone ever did.

The whole country seemed to be Irish on St. Patrick's Day even in 1890:

There wasn't much to-do over St. Patrick's Day in the country but there was in town. There was always the Patrick's Day parade or march. Whether they were Irish or not they'd get in the parade. Even the postman wore green ribbon.

Regarding Valentine's Day:

When we were children they paid more attention to Valentine's Day than now. I remember there was a boy lived back of us and he bought a 'store-bought' valentine and a bought valentine was something for a kid in those days. We usually made our own. The windows would be full of the ugliest valentines and if we didn't like someone we bought the ugliest one we could find and sent it to them. But this boy bought one of these lace-a pretty one with bunches of white here and there on it and he was only about ten or twelve. He gave the valentine to my brother to give to me cause he was too shy and my brother kept holding that valentine about my head and making me promise. No telling how many times I had to black his boots to get it. We had a valentine box at school and sometimes there were nice ones but often they were ugly.

Christmas memories were vague with the exception of religious ceremonies:

We never went to midnight Mass when I was growing up in town but after I was married and living in the country we always went. We drove the five miles to church in a buggy. We'd get home from Mass along about two o'clock in the morning. We'd usually have some people in and we'd all have a big breakfast. It was butchering time and there was always fresh sausage, hams, and buttermilk biscuits. They'd go home when it was daylight. No, we couldn't sleep then on Christmas day. We always had to get up and make a big dinner and the animals had to be fed on time.

I don't remember anything being made for New Years Eve or New Year's Day. Perhaps they did in the city but no one in the country made much of it as they do today.

Kate's experience with her first pair of cherished "spring-heel" shoes:

I had a chum who sat with me in school. Her name was Dora and she was very poor and had a bad reputation for taking things. Mother didn't like me playing with her but I was glad to have a chum and so I did. One day I got to wear my new spring-heel shoes to school and everyone of the girls admired them and at the last recess in the afternoon, just an hour before we went home, Dora talked me into letting her wear them 'til the end of school. I did but when we were let out she ran and I couldn't catch her. I went to her house and told her mother who found her hiding and made Dora give them back. No, it didn't make any difference in our friendship. I know Dora was like that.

Regarding dances in the country:

Some of my girl friends planned to go out into the country to a country-dance and I'd never been to one. I was just fifteen. I didn't know it at the time but Lege [her future husband] and some of his friends who lived in the country were getting up the dance and inviting people from town to come out to it. We rode out in a big van with fringe on it, horse-drawn. Lege was driving the van and I sat right behind him. That's how I met him. He danced and danced with me. It was held in an open place called the Grove. We danced all the good old dances-the quadrille, polka, waltz and schottische. They were beautiful dances but nobody does them anymore. There were square dances, too, and the music was made by two or three fiddles. There was always a caller to tell us what to do though we didn't really need him. Everyone knew the dances. We just needed someone to keep us together, I guess.

She lived at 617 Pawnee from 1891-5 before she moved out (and lived with her brother, Michael) at 609 N. 8th Street to work at the Fort about 1895-7 where she took care of Fred Harvey's wife's mother and later married and raised her family. She worked as a Harvey Girl as a waitress as far as Albuquerque, New Mexico then worked for Mr. Harvey. Leger lived at 5th and Olive while working there, taking care of his grandmother from 1898 to 1900. On 28 November 1900, Kate and Leger Nicholas Mottin Jr. were married at IMAC, Leavenworth, Kansas, with Minnie Cotter and Frank Mottin as witnesses.

Leger had converted to being Catholic as she remembers:

Grandfather Mottin-it used to be spelled Monteau but nobody could say it right and it gave him trouble so he changed it to Mottin-grandfather Mottin came with his third wife up to Kansas. They bought a lot of land which was very cheap at the time and they set it out in grapes. Wine was the only thing they knew anything about and they made wine commercially. They sold it by the barrel. He bought the land from the government. The soldiers from the Fort used to make practice marches west through Granddaughter Mottin's land. It was not unusual to find a buffalo hoof or an arrowhead in the garden. All these things were commonly found in the fields.

There apparently were some disagreements as to where they would live as Leger had not planned to take his new wife back to his father's house where two maiden sisters, a mother and a grandmother were living. Eventually it was agreed that they should have their own small house on the other side of the garden. The Mottin farm was in the family from 1870 to 1929 or 1930 until it was supposedly foreclosed by the bank. This farm was taken by (Dr.) Leger's grandfather who took it from his father, also Leger, and his wife "Munnie" and (Dr.) Leger's mother and her sisters grew up there before they all went various places. Munnie and Leger's children all attended the former Junction School, near Lowemont about 1906-24, then to Leavenworth High (?) or IMAC and finally to St. Mary's Academy, graduating 1920-32. Munnie lost the farm when Leger died on 29 December 1929 and buried in Lowemont, Kansas. It took several months to build the house with four large rooms, a pantry and a screened porch. On their wedding night, they returned to this little house and as they turned out the lights . . .

. . . all the noise you can imagine broke loose. I didn't know what it was and was frightened to death. It turned out to be some of Lege's friends and the men who'd built our little house. They were banging on pans, playing fiddles and Jew's harps-anything to make a racket. I was scared to death and clung to Lege and begged him to make them go away. I'd never heard of this custom but Lege had and he kept laughing. Finally he went out and talked with them. We didn't invite them in. They just wanted to treat so Lege gave them an order to take to town and get whatever they wanted. They wanted a just, of course.

Regarding their first unusual "refrigerator":

It was just a little cave where the water ran through and we kept our milk and butter and things I'd canned in there. A little stream of water ran through it and emptied way down in the pasture somewhere. There must have been a spring in there though I'm not sure. They made a little room around it for us when we were married.

Regarding snakes:

We kept the front of the house in lawn, you know, and here was a snake in the yard one day. Leger was in the fields and I was afraid of it. I ran and got one the screens-we were washing windows-and threw it over the snake to capture it for Lege. Later when he looked it was gone, of course. He laughed and asked why I hadn't gotten the hoe and killed it. I wouldn't have gotten near it and he knew it.

Yes, I've heard of a hoop-snake. I don't know anything about them only that there was such a thing. My husband used to talk about them. They joined themselves-took their tail mouth and turned into a hoop. It could go faster then a horse could run. I never saw one but I know they exist.

Regarding box socials:

We used to have box suppers all the time. We went to them both before and after we were married. Oh, yes, it was all right if someone else's husband bought yours. Everyone did it and understood. It was the custom. Every woman did her best to put good foods in her box. Her name was put on the box and they were kept behind a curtain or partition. The men would bid on them. The auctioneer would hold a box up and brag on it without saying whose it was. A man wouldn't know which was good unless someone had given him a secret word. The auctioneer would brad on the box, of course. Women how had a steady would tell him her box had so-and-so on it. Sometimes men

would get behind and lay tricks by changing the names on the boxes. They would bid and bid and bid. Often a man would know that another man wanted a box and keep bidding until the boxes went as high as three or four dollars-and then it might be the wrong one. It was a very great offence if you refused to eat with the man who bought your box. The money was raised for different things. Once I remember we had a box social to raise money to put a partition in Junction school and have two teachers instead of the one.

Regarding waking the dead among the Irish, Kate remembers:

In the country as in the city when someone died he was waked at home in the parlor. No one got drunk but they did have their toddies [drink made of alcoholic liquor and of water, sweetened and sometimes spiced with cloves]. They all drank all the way around. Everyone came in and sat down all around the room and pretty soon someone would come wit a pitcher full of toddy and fill everyone's cup. They would come early in the evening, find a place to sit and a couple of old cronies [a close friend of chum] to talk with over their toddies and before the evening was over the whole room would be full. It didn't get loud or take on the atmosphere of a party.

It stayed subdued-each one had a chance to add to the tales being told. They recalled people they'd know but I don't remember that they much discussed the dead one. Most people stayed a considerable time, many until morning and the funeral. (The number of carriages in a man's funeral procession was a mark of pride to his family and was subject for comparison). I recall that the cars and buggies stretched back over three hills when we buried Lege.

Regarding Kansas farming:

I remember one time-and you won't believe this-but we were threshing and a storm came up in the north. The storm was coming and the threshers kept going faster all the time hoping to finish before the storm hit. That rain just poured and it QUIT just across the road from our place. You can't believe that. It stopped right at the road and our men went right on threshing and the man across the way couldn't thresh next day because his wheat wasn't dry. Our guardian angel was watching over us.

Katherine lived in El Paso, Texas after 1953; member of St. Patrick's Cathedral and St. Patrick's Altar Society; moved to Kansas City, Missouri and later to El Paso, Texas; d. on 11 January 1974, El Paso; buried Evergreen Alameda Cemetery.

i.   *Katherine Marie Mottin* m1. Hugo Briesh; m2. Maj. William Feaster
ii. *Helen Rose Mottin* m. Earl Francis Brosnahan
iii. *Margaret Fern Mottin*
iv. *Grace Isadora Mottin* m. Gerald Samuel O'Brennan
v.   *Blanche Agnes Mottin* m. Frank J. Guenther

JOHN JOSEPH ROACHE, b. 3 October 1880 Miles City, Montana; bapt. 31 October 1880 at a catholic church, Miles City, Montana; lived at 329 Ann Ave, near Riverview in Fr. Kuhl's parish; buried at St. John's and undertaken by Daniels and Comfort; d. 23 April 1893, Kansas City, Kansas as his obituary reads:

Last election day, John J. Roach, aged 14 years, struck a cartridge in front of the Ryns house with a brick. A piece of the cartridge pierced the boy's eye causing inflammation of the brain and his death last Sunday.

DANIEL O'CONNELL ROACHE, b. 14 March 1882; Miles City, Montana (according to his registration card of 27 April 1942, b. 14 March 1883 Fort Buford, South Dakota); bapt. 24 September 1882 at his parents' ranch Miles City, Montana; lived with sister, Katie, and brother, Michael, at 609 N. 8th and later at 617 Pawnee in 1900; m. Elizabeth Lynch, New York City, 1908; served in World War I as a private and was promoted to Sergeant with the United States and France; fought in the three major battles of the war including Belleau Woods; cited for bravery and decorated with the Croix de Guerre (War Cross) with Palm, by the French, with whom he was serving at the time-acts of heroism involving combat and enemy forces; supposedly went with his half-brother Chet to France and then later returned to New York?; lived in New York City in 1933-5; register 27 April 1942 Philadelphia, Pennsylvania—it described him having a tattoo on his right arm and having a ruddy complexion (reddish color); had been boarding with a family in the rear of 820 Main Street in Dickson City, Pennsylvania. He was walking in the 400 block of Dunmore Street in Dickson City when he was struck by a heavily loaded produce truck. He later died when he arrived at the Mid-Valley Hospital on 20 November 1945. He was removed to the John Wiorkowski Funeral Home, 1126 Main Street in Dickson City. His obituary mentions him having a sister, Lena, and a daughter, Bessie, both of Bronx, New York. He was buried at Priceburg Cemetery. Cemetery is now called Primitive Methodist Church Cemetery of Dickson City, PA.

WILLIAM PATRICK (BERT) ROACHE (James' twin), b. 15/16 January 1884 Fort Leavenworth, Kansas; bapt. 27 January 1884, Fort Lv by Rev. Joannes B. McKune with Jeremiah Cronin and Mary Catherine Curtin as witnesses. On 1902-4, he lived at 307 Lawrence; m. Margaret Dykstra on 24 March 1917 and appeared to have divorced by 1920; retired as a stove mounter; d. 18 July 1949 Leavenworth; buried at Mt. Calvary. Burial papers have him buried to the right of his mother, but he has no headstone.

JAMES ROACHE (William's twin); b./bapt. dates same as his twin; d. 26 June 1884 of Cholera Infantism at their residence of Metropolitan Avenue; buried at Mt. Calvary. Since he was the first person of the family to have died, the cemetery office has no record of the family having bought a plot by that time, and so he was buried at the top of the hill in the abandoned field. His stone hasn't been located yet. The burial stones in this area are bricks which are flush to the ground and practically overgrown by grass.

JOSEPH M. ROACHE, b. 19 January 1889 Fort Leavenworth, Kansas; bapt. 10 March 1889 Leavenworth by Rev. R.B. Groener, Asst. Pastor with Catherine Berry as sponsor. In 1909, worked as a hostler (moved and serviced trains, buses or other vehicles after their regular runs) at the UP roundhouse while living at 216 Pawnee; Enlisted 8 September 1917 World War I, USA as Private, Co. H 353 Inf and Battery F 334th Field Artillery, Company F; d. 20 November 1917, Camp Pike, Arkansas of pneumonia as there was an epidemic that Fall; undertaken by P. H. Ruebel & Company; buried at Fort Leavenworth, plot D1263-C.

Margaret Josephine Kanelly (M2) Daniel Richard Pike

THOMAS CLEVELAND PIKE, b. 19 February 1893 Kansas City, Kansas; bapt. March 1893 by A. Hochmiller, St. Mary's Church, Kansas City, Kansas, Thomas Moran and Katharine Barry were witnesses [St. Mary-St. Anthony Church, 615 N. 7th St., Kansas City, KS 66101]; August 1968, interviewed and featured in city paper, *Personal Recollections of Buffalo Bill*, Tom, Floyd Warden and Clarence Carson, saw Buffalo Bill's Wild West Show more than half a century ago. He once played hooky the last time Buffalo Bill's show was in town. He remembered a huge tent with an open top. He and some other kids always gathered around Bill, who told them a lot of stories. Bill asked Tom one time if the old Pennsylvania house was still here and the First and Last chance Saloon. Tom's mother answered that they were. Tom remembered the "Fort to Fort" road (Fort Leavenworth to Fort Riley) and the Eight-Mile house, which still stands. He said he went to his first dance at that house, which was called LaCaille house, which was northwest of town on what is now Highway 73. Tom remembered Indians of the Wild West show, the staging of the regular Indian raid, bareback riders and Anne Oakley, a crack-shooter. He saw the show "on the reservation" (Fort Leavenworth) about where the Port of Entry is now, fifth and Metropolitan. Sioux Street, which was never more than one block long, running east and west, divided his property and the Fort. "When people ask me how old I am I tell them I played marbles with Buffalo Bill in Sioux Street." Tom had a copy of *Early History of Leavenworth* (by H. Miles Moore) and it belonged to his parents. He mentioned that the freight office of Russell, Majors and Waddell was located at Metropolitan and seventh, but was then Sioux Street. This corner was where the Kansas-Colorado stage line started. Tom once worked for the Great Western Stove Company in town in the 1900s; served World War I, entered Fort Leavenworth, Kansas,

Corporal, 22 April 1918—23 April 1919, 35th Inf, Co E, and Detachment 1st Co, 164th Disciplinary and Barracks Battalion (511-03-5199/SN 1027570); separated, Camp Funston, Kansas; World War I Victory Button (Bronze) and World War I Victory Medal (Defensive Sector); m. Zell Spain, 21 June 1921, Leavenworth; he said that he moved to 711 Metropolitan in 1922 when Sioux Street was vacated and it was paved; he was a molder in 1930 for the same company; d. 10 February 1970, Kickapoo. Both buried at Fort Leavenworth.

i.   *Robert LeRoy Pike* m1. Charlene Gabbert; m2. Dorcille Phillips
ii. *Thomas Clifford "Pick" Pike* m. Evelyn L. Payne

CHARLES FRANCIS "CHET" PIKE, b. 22 April 1894 Kansas City, Kansas; enlisted at Fort Leavenworth in World War I Army 1917 while living at 1116 N. 6th; served 18 September 1917-14 July 1919 as Private (#2068697); separated from 17th T. Corps (Railway), Camp Funston (at or near Fort Riley), Kansas as a Corporal; assigned to 17th T. Corps (Railway); 17th Co. 14th Grand Division T.C. and Camp Pike, Arkansas Demobolization Group, Funston, Kansas; decorations included World War I Victory Bronze and World War I Victory Medal with Battle Clasps for Defensive Sectory. While serving in France, he met Raymonde Lorre/Loure. Their marriage record shows her being from a small village in Cuille, France. After the war, Chet had promised her that he would marry her when they would return to the states. 2 January 1920 Kansas census shows Chet is single and without kids; On 29 May 1920, she sailed on the ship, *La Touraine*, from Le Havre, France to New York. She was 23 at the time. The shipping record lists Mrs. Briand Leonie as the nearest relative or friend from her hometown of Cuille. Chet then arrived in New York on 8 June 1920; m1 on 23 June 1920 by Rev. B. S. Kelly, IMAC with his brother and sister-in-law, Leo and Francis Pike, as witnesses; been rumored that Chet and Raymonde had two boys, their names are unknown. Only a few family members say that they saw them but they were never heard of again. Kansas 1930 census shows Chet living with his parents and one brother but married, no wife or kids are listed. Not long after their marriage, family mention that Raymonde felt homesick and so Chet took her and supposedly their two boys back to France. Chet's half-brother, Daniel Roache, was to have also gone with them. By 1930, Chet worked for the Missouri Pacific Railway; m2 Jane Manning, 22 January 1934,

Platte City, Missouri. I never knew they had children until I found what looked like their baptismal records at St. Joseph's Church, Leavenworth and kept them for a while. It wasn't until some months later when I received an email from one of the daughters stating that she was their child and she was looking for information on her father and that these records did belong to her. She mentioned that her brother, James, had died some years before. Jane Manning's previous marriage was to a Bradley whom they had Jean Marie (Peggy's half-sister). Chet died on 16 December 1973 in Leavenworth and was buried at the Fort's cemetery, plot K 172. The last that was known of Jane was that sometime after she attended her son's burial. Jane died on 20 April 1975 in Leavenworth of emphysema and buried on Easton Hill

Chet and Raymonde:

i.   *boy*
ii. *boy*

Chet and Jane Manning:

iii. *Margaret Jane "Peggy" Pike* m1 Felix Cordova, m2 Spencer Lee Finch
iv. *James Philip Pike*

Robert Emmet Pike, b. 25 November 1895, Leavenworth, by Dr. J. A. Lane; bapt. 5 January 1896, Leavenworth by Rev. T.J. Downey with Peter Carsin and Monahan as sponsors, Sacred Heart, parents lived on South Second Street; worked for Great Western Stove Company and later as locomotive fireman of the Union Pacific Railroads; m. Mamie Katherine Bodenschatz, 8 September 1917, Kansas City, Missouri, but remarried at St. Cassimir, Leavenworth, April 1918. They later divorced about 1924; World War I Army (SN 3472501) entered Fort Leavenworth, Kansas, 28 August 1918-18 December 1918, Private, while living at 1116 N. 6th, Medical Department; separated Fort Benjamin Harrison, Indiana; World War I Victory Medal and World War I Victory Button (bronze); member of the American Legion and the Eagles Lodge; d. 7 July 1972, Leavenworth; buried at Fort Leavenworth, plot P 2855.

i.   *Margaret Josephine Pike* m. David Ezell

Leo Clement Pike Sr., b. 23 November 1897 Leavenworth by Dr. S. B. Langworthy, parents lived at 816 Shawnee; bapt. 9 January 1898; 2 years of high school; enlisted in World War I Army, 16 April 1917 (#917540) at Fort Leavenworth until 29 March 1929; 1920, General Service School Detail; m. Frances Mary Heckman, 6

September 1921 by Father Angelus, St. Joseph's Church, Leavenworth; WW II 30 March 1929-31 March 1946 (25 years), Teacher's College, Fort Leavenworth, retired as MSgt.; decorations and awards include World War I Victory Button (Bronze); World War I Victory Medal; World War II Victory Medal; Honorable Service Lapel Button; Good Conduct Medal; and American Defense Service Medal; National Guard in Federal Service, within 3 months of discharge; worked at the Army Cooperative record clerk at the Kansas State Prison since April 1958; past commander of the Byron H. Mehl American Legion Post No. 23, past Chef de Gare of the 40-8 and member of the Leavenworth County Fish and Game Association. Frances was a past president of the American Legion Auxiliary, member of the 8 and 40 and the Daughters of Isabella; both killed in a vehicle accident on 20 July 1959 in Kansas; buried at Fort Lv with same headstone, plots M 3366 and 3367.

i.   *Leo Clement "Bud" Pike Jr.*
ii. *Mary Margaret Pike* m. Harvey C. Chadbourne

MARGARET PIKE, b. 31 December 1899 Leavenworth by Dr. S. B. Langworthy, parents lived on 617 Pawnee. Sometimes her birth date is seen as 1 January 1900 since she was born so close to this date; it's unknown if she even had a middle name; bapt. 11 February 1900, IMAC; attended Old Immaculate Conception Cathedral Grade School only finishing the 8th grade; m1 John William Becker. There's hardly any information known of Gma Baskas' first marriage, to John William Becker in 1916 but were soon divorced. According to census, John, son of German immigrants, was born in 1897. From 1919-20, John and Margaret lived at 526 Cheyenne when he was a blacksmith helper at William G. Hesse & Son Mfg. Co.; m2 John Burke Baskas (see Baskas tree) and had her last child with (possibly) Jerome "Jerry" Harrison Wolf, but no marriage (see Baskas tree); d. 4 April 1985, Lansing; buried with her second husband, John Baskas, at Mt. Calvary.

Margaret m1 John William Becker:

i.   *Anna Eileen Becker* m1. Hundsacker, m2. William Gregory Schulte
ii. *Lillian Mae Becker* m. Lee E. Hattok Margaret m2 John Burke Baskas:
i.   *John Joseph "Buddy" Baskas*
ii. *Leo Daniel "Blackie" Baskas*
iii. *Francis William Baskas*
iv. *Thomas Emmett Baskas*
v.   *Patrick Jerome Baskas*
vi. *Robert Edward Baskas*

vii. *Margaret Katherine (M.K.) Baskas*
viii. *Ralph Vincent "Porky" Baskas*
ix. *Johanna Marie Baskas*
x. *Michael Charles Baskas*

Margaret (NM) Jerome "Rome" Harrison Wolfe (?):

xi. *James Anthony "Jim" Baskas*

KATE KEANNEALLY AND JAMES BARRY SR.

MARY ELLEN BARRY, b. February 1886 Leavenworth, Kansas; only seen in 1890 and

1900 Kansas census. By 1905, she's not mentioned, she either married or died. If she died, she's not buried in the Barry plot, where is she?

CATHERINE "KATE" BARRY, b. 4 December 1887, Leavenworth, Kansas; bapt. 1 January 1888 IMAC; worked as a domestic at 232 Pottawatomie while living at 608 N. 4th Street from 1903-6; m. Morris/ Maurice Aliff, 1910, b. 1885, Kansas; lived at 12 North Tremont in 1929 Kansas City, Kansas.

i. *Mary Catherine Aliff* m. Swartz

BRIGIT AGNES BARRY, b. 2 February 1890, Leavenworth, Kansas; bapt 20 April 1890, IMAC; worked as

a domestic while living at 608 N. 4th Street in 1905-6; m. Captain William Jerome Snyder, 17 June 1915, Kansas City, Missouri. William, son of Frank and Carrie (Siegle) Snyder, b. 20 July 1884 on his parent's farm home in Leeper, Clarion County, Pennsylvania; enlisted USMC on 12 March 1904 at Pittsburg, Pennsylvania, served four years; discharged 12 May 1908, Camp Columbia, Cuba, then re-enlisted into Company G, 2nd Battalion Engineers; served Army from 12 May 1908 to 31 December 1931; retired after 30 years; member of the Hancock Lodge 331 AF & AM; Scottis Rite Bodies 32nd degree (Fort Leavenworth); Chapter #1 Ancient Toltec Rite, Topeka, Kansas; and Geop E. White Post 56 V.F.W.; d. 13 December 1959, V.A., Lansing. She d. 27 March 1966, Leavenworth. Both are buried at Fort Leavenworth Cemetery with separate stones. They had no children.

MARGARET ELIZABETH BARRY, (birth record at Leavenworth Public Library shows her mother's maiden name was possibly Wilson?) b. 10 July 1892, Leavenworth, Kansas; bapt. 23 August 1892, IMAC; m. Henry Pickering, 9 November 1903, Leavenworth; worked as a domestic at 328 Ottawa while living at 610 N. 4th Street. He worked as a foreman in a flourmill in Kansas

City, Kansas. They lived at 11 North Tremont in Kansas City in 1929; d. October 1970, Kansas?

i. *William E. Pickering Sr.* m. Josephine B.
ii. *Ruth T. Pickering* m. Raymond West
iii. *Agnes Pickering* m. Duffy

JAMES HENRY BARRY JR., b. 18 September 1894, Leavenworth, Kansas; lived at 608 N. 4th with his family. He and his wife owned and ran the Barry Tavern for more than fifty years where they resided on 601 North 3rd (and Ottawa Street); retired in 1978; m. Florence Belle Hamblin, 9 July 1917, Leavenworth, b. 5 August 1898, Leavenworth. On Wednesday, 4 January 1961, about 8 in the morning, Florence was severely burned over a large portion of her body when her housecoat accidentally was ignited by a cooking stove in her kitchen as she was preparing breakfast. The kitchen was located in the rear of the tavern; d. 9 January 1981 St. John's Hospital, Leavenworth. Both were buried at Mt. Calvary.

i. *James P. Barry* m. Peggy
ii. *Howard Frederick Barry* m. Mary Magdalen Heitlinger

CHAPTER VII

GENERATION 2

Researcher
Richard S. Baskas

FRANK JOSEPH BASKAS AND ANNIE MARIE KILLILAY

MARIE BASKAS, b. 22 February 1894, Leavenworth, Kansas; m. Clarence John DeWoody (also m. Charles Lord 31 December 1919, according to marriage record?). They were found in 1934 and 1936 Kansas City, Kansas directories. Their obituary mentions they were found dead at their home of 1323 Minnesota Avenue on 28 November 1937 in Kansas City, Kansas. The couple was discovered in their night clothing the night prior by an employee of the Whipple Radio Company at 1321 of the same street, just east of their home. The responding police found all doors and windows locked. A gas stove was going full blast. Early supposition was that the couple had died asphyxiation as the result of the stove consuming all the oxygen in the room. However a puzzling element was added when the officers found a cat in the room alive. The couple worked at the Linwood Ice Cream Company plant of 325 Linwood Blvd. The couple had worked there for 15 years. Their obituary mentions them having a son who recently left for a CCC camp. Research indicates they had no children together, just his from a previous. His petition for administration lists George De Woodey (brother), Velma May McDonald (sister, Harrisonville,

Missouri), and a nephew De Woodey. Her petition lists Frank Baskas (brother, Los Angeles), Thomas J. Baskas (brother, Brooksfield, Texas), Walter Baskas (brother, Tremont Hotel, Leavenworth) and James Baskas (brother, Havensville, Kansas); both buried at Mt. Calvary.

FRANCIS JOSEPH BASKAS, (569-01-7823), b. 2 January 1898, Leavenworth, Kansas; bapt. 6 January 1898, IMAC; registered (lived at 523 Short St, Lv at time) World War I, 1918; worked at Camp Eustis, Lee Hall, Virginia; Army Vet (#39254089), World War II as a Private, 28 July 1942-5 July 1943; assignments and geographical locations, DEML Sec SCU 1918; entered at San Diego, California and separated in North Little Rock, Arkansas; decorations included World War II Victory Medal and Lapel Button; lived at Havensville, Kansas for 20 years before moving to Leavenworth; d. 16 May 1977, Kansas; buried at V.A. Cemetery, plot 40-14-55 (have stone).

THOMAS JOSEPH BASKAS, b. 9 May 1900, Leavenworth, Kansas; only completed 8 years of school; registered (serial #3330) World War I, 1919 (lived at 523 Short St) served Camp Eustis, Virginia; enlisted 27 September 1945 for Hawaiian Department, Air Corps;

Army Vet in France Field, Canal Zone, Panama in the 1940s; lived in Reno since 1945 where he was a desk clerk at the Overland hotel. The hotel closed on 31 March 1977 and was bought by Harrah's and later became a parking lot. The hotel was put on the Nevada State Register of Historic Sites on 4 November 1999; m1 Mickey; m2 Mary Ruth Pistorius, hostess at the Gold N Silver and the Pagoda Restaurants. She had been living here since 1953; d. 20 March 1976, Reno, Nevada; both buried at Mountain View Cemetery, Reno (need stones).

WALTER WILLIAM BASKAS, b. 4 July 1903, Leavenworth, Kansas; bapt. 3 August 1903, Leavenworth, sponsored by Josie Wencel and William McCann. His parents were living at 5th and Pawnee at the time; only attended 8 years of schooling quitting at age 15; worked as a Boring Mill Operator for 10 years at Great Western Mfg. Co. and 15 years as a bartender; enlisted (lived at 513 Delaware), Navy on 26 November 1920, Kansas City, Missouri as a rank of F 3/c for 2 years; listed 523 Short Street and his Uncle John Killilay as next of kin. He was honorably discharged 44 days prior to end of his term from the U.S.S. New York as F2cat San Pedro, California for government convenience; enlisted again on 20 April 1942 for 2 years in Kansas City, Missouri as rank of Coxswain, class V-6 and served from 7 May 1942 to 6 February 1945 at Santa Cruz, California; reported from Kansas City, Missouri on 10 May 1942 to NTS, NOB, Norfolk, Virginia in a construction company; transferred to Advance Base Depot, Hueneme, California on 5 June 1942; became BM2c on 1 February 1943; service # 3411421 (511-03-5555); (M1) Darlene Hutchinson 8 November 1946 Leavenworth; (M2) Lois Darlene Hubbard (same person?) 3 June 1949 Leavenworth; painter at Wadsworth V.A. Center for more than 12 years, retired in 1972; d. 31 October 1990 Leavenworth of appendicitis; buried at V.A. National Cemetery, plot 42-22-5 (have stone). Lois, b. 22 September 1919 Orilla, Iowa, daughter of Clarence M. and Gretchen M. (Phillips) Haynes; (M1) Homer Hubbard 1938, d. 1946; president of the Golden Age Seniors and the Friendship Club, and a member of the Salvation Army women's group "Happy Faces"; d. 15 November 2004 Leavenworth; buried Glendale Cemetery Des Moines, Iowa.

i. *"Scooter" Baskas*

ANNA "ANNIE" JOSEPHINE BASKAS, b. 3 April 1904, Leavenworth, Kansas; bapt. 26 April 1904, Kansas; d. 23 May 1909, Leavenworth; buried at Mt. Calvary (have stone).

JAMES "JIMMY" BASKAS (FITZPATRICK), b. 15 January 1906, Leavenworth, Kansas by Dr. C.K. Vaughn. His parents were living at 5th and Cheyenne at the time. Jimmy was orphaned at an early age. A priest brought him from a Kansas City orphanage where he would be sponsored by Mr. Fitzpatrick, a farmer northeast of Onaga. Jimmy made no sacraments, according to Father Michael Stubbs, whose name appeared in the register at that time. Jimmy worked several years for his sponsor, becoming a farmer, and then later took his name. Mr. Fitzpatrick willed his farm to several relatives and after his death. Jimmy remained on the farm and eventually bought out the relatives. He never married. Leon Becker, who lived across the street from the cemetery, mentioned that her husband and Jim Cline (who is buried at cemetery) had cared for Jimmy while he lived at the shack on Parallel Road. He then supposedly lived in a nursing home until his death. Jimmy was a member of St. Vincent DePaul Catholic Church at Onaga; d. 27 December 1990, Onaga Community Hospital; buried Coal Creek Community, north of Onaga (have stone).

ELIZABETH BASKAS AND
MICHAEL F. GLYNN

HELEN GLYNN, b. 17 December 1900, Leavenworth, Kansas by Dr. W. W. Walter with parents living at 570 2nd Ave.; m. George Meeker (family mentions his last name originally Cassidy, from his biological father?), b. 1890 Kansas, Pool Hall Manager (Meeker & Leo B. Donovan) on 404-406 Cherokee, lived at 1209 S. 2nd in 1930; d. 12 December 1995, Hampton, Virginia, buried Oakland Cemetery, Hampton, Virginia (**need stone**).

i.   *Marie Elynor Meeker*
ii. *Robert E. Meeker* m. Pat E.
iii. *Patricia M. Meeker* m. Cecil Grimm Mauld

BLANCHE C. GLYNN, b. 20 February 1902, Leavenworth, Kansas; m. John D. Becher 3 September 1925; retired from V.A. Center, 1966; member of St. Joseph Carmelite Church and the Daughters of Isabella; d. 30 March 1976 Leavenworth County Convalescent Infirmary; buried Mt. Calvary, Lansing, Kansas; John owned and ran the 7-Up Bottling Company in Leavenworth; John b. 1900, d. 23 March 1977 Leavenworth (**no stones**). The home farm on which William was born has been in the family of John and Christine (Hombach)Becherfor6generations.

John b. 1820 on the same farm, son of Pether Becher, b. 1785. Pether was a farmer and stockman and during the Napoleonic war fought under Napoleon, in Russia. John at first rented land from Feerst Van Hartzfeld, later owning his own farm. Christine (Hombach), b. on neighboring farm in 1823, m. John 1848, she d. 1876. They had 7 children, John, Mary Ann, Catherine and Peter (all deceased), William, John and Henry (both in Germany). William attended public schools up to 8th grade. He remained at home and worked on the farm until he was 26. He sailed from Bremen, Germany on 14 May 1884 and landed in Baltimore, Maryland on 28 May 1884 where he later located to Leavenworth. William Becher, b. 5 August 1857, Wisseen, Coblinz, Germany. Joseph Riepenkroger and William opened a soda water bottling works in Leavenworth at 736 Seneca shortly before the turn of the century. On 1892, he started his own factory for soda water, pops and ginger ales. He built a building 60 by 30 feet of brick with most modern machinery. He kept this up to the finest efficiency for years, replacing outworn and old fashioned machinery with newest and best. He was able to make 300 cases a day. Operating as Becher and Riepenkroger and later as Becher & Company, it produced ginger ale, sarsaparilla and assorted flavored soft drinks. Peter Haag later became a partner and later changed to Becher and Haag. Haag left in 1933 to open a beer distributorship and in 1939, Becher entered the bottling works on a fulltime basis. Here he worked for the city for 18 days at the brewery. On 1 August, he worked at the Soda Water Works for 4 years. When he closed on 1 January 1967, it marked the end of the last remaining bottling works in Leavenworth. He m. Frances Riepenkrooger 15 May 1888 Leavenworth. Frances' father and his 2 brothers came to the states at New Orleans to St. Louis where they remained for one year. They were shoemakers and in 1857 came to Leavenworth in 1902. His wife d. same year and both buried in Leavenworth. They had 11 children. William and Frances had William (then at Chicago), Mary (Atchinson, Kansas), Henry (Leavenworth), Joseph, John, Leona, Francis, Angela, Alois (twin) and Peter (twin and deceased at the time). All were living in Leavenworth at the time. William and family were members of St. Joseph's Catholic Church and he was member of Fraternal Order of Eagles and Republican.

i. *Blanche M. Becher* m. Raymond Joseph Lippman Sr.

JOSEPH "BOOTS" LAWRENCE GLYNN, SR., (511-03-5575) b. 3 August 1905, Leavenworth, Kansas by Dr. C. K. Vaughn; lived with sister, Helen, and her family on 1209 S. 2nd as a grocery store clerk in 1930; m1 Barbara J.; she had child from previous

and he adopted baby when both got married; m2 Alice L. "Cy" (Cook) Glynn 17 May 1975 Sacramento, California; Cy b. 1911, d. 9 August 1980; retired Production Contractor at McClellan AFB; d. 16 August 1981 Sacramento, California; buried Internment Calvary Cemetery (**need stone**).

i. *Jean Ellen (Joanne?) Glynn* m. Harris
ii. *William Glynn*
iii. *Jerome Glynn*
iv. *Ronald Glynn*
v. *Barbara Glynn* m. Packard
vi. *Joseph Lawrence Glynn Jr.* m. Jacquelyn

JOHN WALTER GLYNN SR., b. 18 December 1907, Atchinson, Kansas; m. Dorothy Alice Martin, 22 December 1935 Kansas; Dorothy worked for Southwestern Bell telephone company in Leavenworth, member of Knight Capers of St. Joseph Catholic Church and member of Southwestern Bell's Pioneer Club, she b. 27 October 1909 Easton, Kansas, d. 22 July 1991 Hampton, Virginia; d. 19 January 2001, Charlottesville,

Virginia; buried Easton Cemetery, Kansas.

i. *John Walter Glynn Jr.* m. Barbara Anne Bachman
ii. *Linda Sue Glynn* m. David William Hutchinson

GENEVIEVE GLYNN, b. 9 February 1909, Leavenworth, Kansas by Dr. C. K. Vaughn with parents living at 1209 S. 2nd ; after her mother died, she was adopted by John and Jennie Perry where she attended schools in Kansas City, Missouri; m. Leo W. Burns, 16 August 1940 Liberty, Missouri; member of Altar Society and American Legion Auxiliary and the 8 and 40; retired from the Fort as secretary in engineering department; d. 18 April 1987, Leavenworth; buried Wadsworth Cemetery, 41A-18-2; Leo, b. 1 August 1911 Leavenworth; graduated from IMAC and attended Bendictine College while playing football; served in Army Air Corps during WW II; retired as fire chief; Leo d. 5 July 2007 Leavenworth; they had no children; both buried V.A. Cemetery.

J.W. (JOSEPH WILLIAM?) BASKAS AND VIOLET MCNEIL

CLARENCE JOSEPH BASKAS, b. 13 November 1904 Leavenworth by Dr. S. L. Oxford; d. 4 April 1906

Leavenworth/Lansing; buried Mt. Calvary Cemetery (**need stone**).

JOHN BURKE BASKAS AND MARGARET PIKE

JOHN "BUDDY" JOSEPH BASKAS SR., b. 17 December 1921, Leavenworth; bapt. 1 January 1922; served Navy in Pacific from San Francisco, California to Treasure Island; m. Mary Margaret "Mary Margaret" Crook, 23 April 1954, Kansas. Mary b. 25 March 1924, Leavenworth, bapt. 4 May 1924 Sacred Heart. Buddy spent 45 months as a security guard on the Merchant Marine ships in World War II USN, seeing action in the Pacific and Atlantic; worked briefly at the Fort's commissary, Sherman Army Air Field and the Veterans Affairs Center; began his 27-year career at the U.S. Federal Penitentiary beginning as a security guard and ending as a plumber; worked briefly as a plumbing inspector for Leavenworth. Mary Margaret d. 13 January 2004, Colonial Manor, Lansing; Buddy d. 14 June 2005, at his home Leavenworth; both buried at Mt. Calvary.

i. *Pamela Ann Baskas* m. Ronald E. Jones
ii. *Angela Marie Baskas* m. Eugene Everett Hacker

iii. *Kathy Lee Baskas* m. Mike Goldak

iv. *John Joseph "Skip" Baskas* m. Sharon Fevurly

LEO DANIEL "BLACKIE" BASKAS, b. 3 January 1924, Leavenworth; served on a boat in Army in California; d. 8 July 1997, Leavenworth; m. Mildred Overman/ Eubanks, b. 16 April 1930, Pueblo, Colorado, d. 30 April 1999, and cremated; Sergeant, World War II USA; bartender until retirement; life member of VFW and American Legion; buried at V.A. Cemetery plot 47-16-52.

i. *Leo Daniel "Danny" Baskas* m. Yolanda Louise Martinez

ii. *Rita Marie "Kitty" Baskas* m. Charles Albro Stine

iii. *William Anthony Baskas* m. Joan Reed

FRANCIS "FRANK" WILLIAM BASKAS, b. 9 April 1926, Leavenworth; bapt. 25 April 1926, Kansas; Cathedral Grade School '39; IMAC School '44; World War II USN in Japan on USS Flint, until 1946 and Korean War; 24 December 1946, m. Louetta "Lou" Katherine Kenny, Leavenworth, b. 1 October 1929, d. 11 October 1998 Leavenworth, member of Lady Knights of Columbus and VFW Auxiliary; members of the St. Patrick's Parade in Leavenworth for 14 years. Due to their continued support, they were Grand Marshals on their last parade; d. 21 July 2005 Kansas City, Kansas. Both buried Mt. Calvary.

i. *Terri Lou Baskas* m1. Mike Bielka; m2. McManms; m3. Teavebaugh

THOMAS "TOM" EMMETT BASKAS, b. 5 September 1928, Leavenworth; m. Wilda June Snider 22 December 1955, Kansas City, Missouri; June, b. 27 May 1928 Oak Hill, Illinois, d. 2 March 1996 Peoria, Illinois; retired from Illinois Furniture Company in 1989; d. 24 August 1991, Pekin, Illinois; both buried at Southport Cemetery, Oak Hill, Illinois. (**need stone**)

i. *Linda Kay Baskas* m. Tim J. Berger

PATRICK "PAT" JEROME BASKAS, b. 1 January 1931, Leavenworth; only person who was drafted, only served a year then let out on medical discharge; m. Dorothy Mae Petit, 25 September 1954, b. 26 May 1932. Their reception was held at Lee and Lilly Mae Hattok's house that was once in Lansing; USMC; helped build the Missouri River Bridge by putting in the concrete pillars in the ground and river. They had no children.

ROBERT "BOBBY" EDWARD BASKAS, b. 8 May 1933, Kickapoo; m. Vivian

"Tudy" Rose Heitlinger, 8 June 1957, St. John's, Leavenworth, b. 15 June 1931 Leavenworth, d. 20 May 2004 Leavenworth; USN 24 November 1952-16 November 1956 as SN in Brownsville, Texas on USS Rio Grande. They had no children but raised Tudy's from a previous. Tudy buried at Leavenworth National, plot 57-11-36.

i.   *Vivian Lee Baskas* m. Robert Tracey Berg Sr.
ii. *Sharon Louise Baskas* m. Clarence Albert Filbert

MARGARET "M.K." KATHERINE BASKAS, b. 8 June 1935, Kickapoo; IMAC '53; served 6 years in WAVES, Navy's all women's military; basic training in Bainbridge, Maryland; Charlestown, South Carolina; Great Lakes, Illinois; Oahu, Hawaii (basketball) and Anacostia, D.C.; Retired from American Automobile Association in Falls Church, Virginia, then was transferred and in Heathrow, Florida and so did she and family until she retired in 1992 in Florida; remained single and raised Richard Scott (book author) and James Allen, her nephews.

RALPH "PORKY" VINCENT BASKAS, b. 15 August 1936, Leavenworth; m1 Catherine Martin; 25 June 1956; m2 JoAnn Shasick (sister to Una Mae Shasick, wife of Michael Baskas); USN; buried Mt. Calvary.

Ralph and JoAnn:

i.   *Michelle Renee Baskas* m. Thomas Benjamin Portenier Jr.

JOHANNA MARIE BASKAS, b. and d., 27 January 1940, Leavenworth; buried next to her mother at Mt. Calvary.

MICHAEL CHARLES BASKAS SR., b. 26 March 1943 Leavenworth; IMAC '61; m. Una Mae Shasick, 19 November 1966; A.A., Fort Scott Community College, Kansas; retired Plant Foreman, Leavenworth, began driving school bus.

i.   *Kimberly Lynn Baskas*
ii. *Michael Charles Baskas Jr.* m1. Julie L. Hartman; m2. Jamie Sotomayor

JAMES "JIM" ANTHONY BASKAS (WOLF), b. 21 March 1945 St. John's Hospital Leavenworth and was named by a nun; First Holy Communion 25 April 1954 IMAC; Confirmation 26 February 1956 IMAC; only attended Old Immaculata Conception Grade School from 1952-61. He quit school to support his mother and himself. One of the jobs he had in early 1960s was working at the old Kaaz woodworking building, on Delaware between 2nd and 3rd Street. The wood that he made was used to make the altar at the Immaculate Conception Church. It wouldn't be until sometime after John Baskas had passed away that Jim would begin to learn of his real last name [An old family friend of the Baskas knew for years eventually told my father this story]. John used to show off to his friend, saying that there was a wolf in the house (he was talking about my father, who was a baby then). John had many animals that he was razing at the Pawnee house. After a few minutes of trying to actually find a wolf, the fried finally caught on and realized that it was the baby that John was talking about. This is when the friend realized that the baby wasn't of the Baskas name, but the Wolf name.

Before my parents were married, they lived across the street from each other in Leavenworth. My father had enlisted into the Navy and had begun going through basic training at San Diego, California. He said he was there in November, the same month that President Kennedy was shot. But for some strange reason, my father was found not fit for military and was discharged. He had spent one day shy of a month in the military. Soon after, on 27 February 1964, he married my mother, Betty Emma Karnes. About a year after their marriage, they decided to move to Merced, California. My mother's mother had moved there some years ago where she had been living with one of her daughters (my mother's sister). My grandmother had mentioned to my parents of a job in Merced and so they moved. Their first child, me, was born in Merced. Shortly after I was born, my father quit that job and my parents would return to Leavenworth. A few years later, my brother would be born in Leavenworth. From 1966-77, Jim was a firefighter for Leavenworth. Ironically, he would be the last person in the family to be part of history. He was part of the team to have fought the fire that destroyed what was then St. John's Hospital in 1974. Not many years later, my parents would divorce. My mother then remarried to an Army guy from Fort Leavenworth and he would be stationed in San Antonio, Texas before she would late join the Army. My father m2 Marrianne Margaret Lane in Leavenworth. My brother and I would live with them for a few years it seemed before we were adopted about 23 March 1974. My father and his wife would then move to and lived in Minnesota for some years. Unfortunately that marriage ended and he returned to Leavenworth where sometime later m3 Virginia Marie Heintzelman 22 December 1999 Leavenworth.

James and Betty:

i.   *Richard Scott Baskas*
ii.   *James Allen Baskas*

MARY ELLEN "NELL" ROACHE AND PATRICK LEO CANTWELL

EDWARD PATRICK CANTWELL, b. 6 September 1896, Leavenworth; bapt. with Katherine Roache and James Fitzgerald as witnesses; d. 14 March 1899, Blaine, Kansas of typhoid pneumonia.

MARGARET KATHERINE CANTWELL, b. 1 May 1898 [Dewy Day?] Leavenworth, Kansas; bapt. with Michael B. Roache and Katherine Cotter as witnesses; m. Charles Joseph Arnold, 14 June 1922, St. Patrick's Cathedral, El Paso, Texas with Katherine Mottin and George Arnold as witnesses; d. 17 December 1988, El Paso.

i.   *Mary Margaret Arnold* m. Michael J. Devlin Jr.
ii.   *Charlotte Josephine Arnold* m. William Lee Sitton
iii. *Bernice Threasa Arnold* m. Charles Elwin Haskins

PATRICK LEO CANTWELL, (185-03-5268) b. 22 July 1901 Leavenworth, Kansas; bapt. with Delia Cantwell (Mrs. J. Doyle) and Frank Desmond as witnesses; m. Margaret Hennessey, 13 January 1929, Amarillo, Texas by Justice of the Peace; d. 18 November 1975 Los Angeles, California.

VINCENT BERNARD CANTWELL, b. 27 May 1903 Leavenworth, Kansas; bapt. with Mr. and Mrs. Leger Mottin as witnesses; m. Lillian Arron, 17 January 1931, Las Cruces, New Mexico by Justice of the Peace; d. 1 January 1969, El Paso, Texas

FRANCIS JOSEPH CANTWELL, b. 24 January 1905 Leavenworth, Kansas; bapt. with Mrs. Leger Mottin and Joe Cantwell as witnesses; m. Madeline Seibert, 14 August 1937, Sante Fe, New Mexico; d. 23 November 1981, Albuquerque, New Mexico.

i.   *John Anthony Cantwell*
ii.   *Ellen Cantwell*
iii. *Kenneth Cantwell*
iv.   *Ann Cantwell*

MARY GERALDINE CANTWELL, b. 25 December 1906 Leavenworth, Kansas; bapt. with Mr. and Mrs. Daniel Richard Pike as witnesses; (m1-eloped enroute to Cloudcroft) to Leonard Wilson Brown, 6 September 1925; m2 Robert L. Flynn on 13 November 1948 El Paso, Texas; d. 28 July 2004 Veterans Hospital, Tucson, Arizona.

i.   *Geraldine Patricia Brown* m. Richard Chester Wheelock

JOHN LILLIS CANTWELL, (453-05-9748) b. 12 July 1908 Leavenworth, Kansas; bapt. with (Aunt) Maggie Cantwell and (Uncle) Joe Roache as witnesses; m. Mary Virginia Cowles, 3 July 1933, Las Cruces, New Mexico by Rev. Buchanan; retired hardware salesman; d. 1 February 1995 El Paso, Texas.

ROBERT EMMET SYDNEY CANTWELL, b. 20 January 1912, High Prairie, Kansas; bapt. Sacred Heart with Thomas C. Pike and Margie Pike as witnesses; d. 10 July 1913, El Paso of dysentery.

KATHERINE MARGARET "MUNNIE" ROACHE AND LEGER MOTTIN

KATHERINE MARIE MOTTIN, b. 13 October 1901, Lowemont farm, Kansas; bapt. 10 November 1901, St. Joseph's, Lowemont, Kansas, sponsored by Jules Mottin and Maria Cotter; worked for the Harvey's at the home; St. Mary's Academy, 1919-(1920 yearbook) 28 September: Reading-*The Man in the Shadow*, Kingsley; In Honor of St. Cecilia, 22 November: Vocal Solo-*Just As I Am*, Danks; Complimentary to The Rev. J.H. Reading; 21 January: Reading-*Her Rival*, Anon; Sacred Concert 11 April: Duet (w/ Mabel Hutsing)-*O Divine Redeemer*, Gounod; Virgilia

1 June: Katherine as Virgilia; In Honor of the Alumnae 10 June: *The Spider and the Fly*, Brooks; Distinguished in Intermediate Piano; (M1) Hugo Briesh, El Paso, Texas, 24 September 1924 with Mr. and Mrs. George Arnold as witnesses; (M2) Major William Feaster; d. 8 January 1975, Kansas City, Missouri.

Katherine and Hugo:

i.   *Paul Briesh*
ii. *Mary Katherine (Mary Kay) Briesh*

HELEN ROSE MOTTIN, b. 28 October 1903, Lowemont farm, Kansas; bapt. 14 November 1903, St. Joseph's, Lowemont, Kansas, sponsored by Patrick Cantwell and Helen Cantwell; St. Mary's Academy, 1921-(1920 yearbook) 28 September: Piano Solo-*Sprites of the Glen*, Dennee; In Honor of St. Cecilia 22 November: Violin Duet (w/ Eileen McCallion)-*Vision*, Von Blon; 29 February: Violin Solo-*Andantino*, Kreisler; Graduate Recital, 22 April: Piano-*Scene de Ballet*, De Beriot; Piano-*Somewhere a Voice is Calling*, Tate; Distinguished in Intermediate Violin; Choral; Latin III; Algebra III; Literature; Rhetoric; Composition, Academic I; Spelling; Medieval and Modern History; Physical Training-Fourth

Hour Class; (1921 yearbook) 5 December: Etiquette for Ancestors, English IV; 27 February: Reading-*The Dancing Lesson*, Tarkington; *As You Like It*: 1 June-as Phebe, a shepherdess; Honors of Graduation-Classical Course; Gold Medal for Best Essay; Excellence in Drawing; Intermediate Piano; Intermediate Violin; Composition; Oral Expression (First Year); Physical Training; m. Earl Francis Brosnahan Sr., St. Joseph's, Lowemont, 26 November 1924. Earl, b. 1 March 1897 Knobnoster, Missouri, d. 30 January 1963, Prairie Village, Kansas, ran their third generation heavy construction company, Brosnahan Brothers, with his brother and father. They lived in Kansas City, Missouri, raised their family, and were active in St. Peter's parish. All she ever wanted to do in life was to raise her children. Her children and the home were the center of her life. She sewed beautifully, played the piano, baked for many church bake sales and passed on to her children the value of education. She took Latin for 4 years at the Academy and won the Latin Medal. At age 65, she took classes at Johnson County Community College. She lives in Overland Park, Kansas until her death, 16 January 2008; burial Leavenworth.

i. *Helen DeSalme "Sammy" Brosnahan* m. Lewis Johnston Vaughan

ii. *Catherine Ann Brosnahan*

iii. *Earl Francis Brosnahan* m. June Therese Mullen

iv. *(Dr.) Leger Nicholas Mottin Brosnahan* m. (Dr.) Irene Mayshir Teoh

v. *Mary Virginia Brosnahan* m. (Dr.) Benjamin D. McCallister

vi. *Roger Paul Brosnahan* m. Jill Ann Farley

vii. *John Joseph Brosnahan* m. Marilyln Puiung Chow

MARGARET FERN MOTTIN, b. 18 May 1905, Lowemont farm, Kansas; bapt. St. Joseph's Lowemont; St. Mary's Academy, 1923-(1920 yearbook) 25 January: Piano Solo-Pantomime, Moszkowski; Sacred Concert 11 April: Accompanist; St. Mary's Choral; Distinguished in Intermediate Piano; Elementary Certificate in Art Progressive Series of Piano Lessons; Distinguished in Musical Theory; Choral; French I; Latin I; Algebra I; Literature, Academic I; Rhetoric; Composition; Spelling (1921 yearbook) 27 February: Piano Solo—Prelude in G Minor, Op. 23, No. 5, Rachmaninoff; Graduation Recital: 24 April-pianist; Excellence in Drawing, Advanced Piano, Spelling (1923 yearbook) Pianist: Chaconne, Bach-Busoni; Allegro-"Vienna Carnival Scene",

Opus 26, Schumann; Adagio Cantabile-"Sonata Pathetique", Opus 13, Beethoven; Prelude in G Minor, Opus 23, No. 5, Rachmaninoff; Bolero, Opus 19, Chopin; Nocturne, Opus 15, No. 2; Chopin; Etude, Opus 10, No. 12; Chopin; First Movement from Concerto in D Minor, Opus 15, Brahms; The Bohemian Girl (opera): played Nobles; moved to El Paso, Texas in 1926 to take on a job; Vice President of R. Hoover & Company, Inc. (Cotton Brokers) which was later owned by Hohenberg/Cargill. She retired from that company after 50 years; member of St. Patrick's Cathedral, St. Patrick's Altar Society, Ladies of Charity and Chamber of Commerce Women's Department and the Woman's Auxiliary, UTEP; volunteer at Sierra Hospital from 1976-8 and was on the Board of Volunteer Association; d. 26 June 1995, El Paso; buried in Evergreen Alameda Cemetery. She remained single.

GRACE ISADORA MOTTIN, b. 26 February 1907, Lowemont farm, Kansas; bapt. St. Joseph's Lowemont; St. Mary's Academy 1925-Advertising Manager "The Pine" '25; The Bohemian Girl (opera):played gypsies '23;Baseball '22-'23; Basketball '22-'25; Cercle Francais '22; Choral '22-'25; Class President '23-'24; Dramatic Art

'25; soon after worked at Shubert Theatre in Kansas City, Missouri; m. Gerald Samuel O'Brennan, 2 January 1936 at St. Patrick's, El Paso; raised their four children here; Gerald was educator and she was legal secretary for law firm of Mayfield and Broaddus; investigated adoptions for a County judge; after retirement, volunteered for several hospitals, hospice work and numerous church-sponsored efforts to serve the needy; Gerald d. 1981; d. 22 December 2006 Spearman, Texas; buried Fort Bliss National Cemetery, El Paso.

i.   *Brian Leger O'Brennan*
ii. *Gerald Alan O'Brennan*
iii. *Mary Andrea O'Brennan* m. Mark Moulton
iv. *Rosemary O'Brennan* m. Wade Bailey Parks

BLANCHE AGNES MOTTIN, b. 20 April 1912, Lowemont farm, Kansas; bapt. St. Joseph's, Lowemont; St. Mary's Academy 1929-President '28-'29; Spanish Club '27, Secretary '28, Vice-President '29; Choral '27-'29; Athletics '27-'29; Dramatics '27-'29; Sejulit, Treasurer '28-'29; A. M. C. Club '27; Sodality '27-'28, Treasurer '29; Operetta '27-'29; Johnson County Community College, Overland Park, Missouri '31; m. Frank J. Guenther, d. 3 June 1968; They had no children; worked as a nurse; d. 5 January 1999, El Paso, Texas.

THOMAS CLEVELAND PIKE AND ZELL SPAIN

ROBERT LEROY PIKE, b. 18 January 1924, Leavenworth; bapt. 18 January 1924, Leavenworth; World War II overseas, Corporal Technician 5th Grade with a motor pool detachment; enlisted 27 February 1945 (#37511640), Fort Leavenworth—24 October 1945 at Fort Benning, Georgia; served again 10 June 1948—21 September 1949 as a Corporal, serving in 5025 Area SVC Unit Stat Complement Mil Pol Det CMP White PD Washington, D.C.; made Leavenworth his home until he moved to Murdock, Nebraska three months prior to his death; accidentally electrocuted at a rock quarry at Kerford Quary near South Bend, Indiana. He was a truck driver and had stopped at the quarry. As he was walking near a large motor, he turned to answer to a call and slipped against an iron guardrail that was shorted; m1 Charlene Gabbert; m2 Dorcille Phillips; d. 24 July 1953, South Bend, Indiana; buried Fort Leavenworth with military honors.

Robert and Charlene:

i.   *Constance Jean Pike*

Robert and Dorcille:

ii. *Roberta Kathleen "Bobbie" Pike* m. Charley Shoemaker

THOMAS "PICK" CLIFFORD PIKE, b. 11 March 1930 Leavenworth; Retired Army 1950's of 20 ½ years; retired from Hallmark Cards of 20 years; former member of Leavenworth Umpires Association and officiated sports for more than 40 years; member of Eagles Aerie No. 55, VFW and American Legion; d. 7 May 2009 Leavenworth; m. Evelyn L. Payne, 7 June 1952, Platte City, Missouri, d. 8 March 1999, Leavenworth; served in Vietnam War. She was a member of the V.F.W., American Legion and Eagles Auxiliaries; avid bingo player and instrumental in providing bingo games to patients to the V.A. Medical Center throughout her involvement with the American Legion. She worked for McCormack, Payton Moving and Storage for 20 years. She began as a packer and later moved in the office; both buried Fort Leavenworth.

i.   *Robert Lee Pike* m. Lori
ii. *Janet Pike* m. Carter

CHARLES FRANCIS "CHET" PIKE AND RAYMONDE LORRE

TWO PIKE BOYS, 2 January 1920 Kansas census shows Chet is single and without kids; According to Dorothy Baskas' grandmother's diary, "Ches Pike got married to Miss Frienche on 23rd day of June 1920. Chet has got two children already." 1930 census shows Chet living with his parents but married, no wife or kids are listed.

CHARLES FRANCIS "CHET" PIKE AND JANE MANNING

MARGARET "PEGGY" JANE PIKE, b. 13 November 1934 Leavenworth; bapt. 2 December 1934, IMAC with Lillian Becker as witness. Since her mother was getting sick, she and her brother were soon adopted by Hugo Gustov and Philena Holmgren of Onaga, Kansas, but were later raised by Leonard and Bessie Barker; graduated from high school in Wheaton, Kansas in 1952; m1 (later annulled) Felix Cordova; m2 Spencer Lee Finch.

Peggy and Felix:

i. *Dennie Rae Cordova (Barker)* m. Nancy

Peggy and Spencer:

ii. *Paul Samuel Finch* m. Nancy Lyn Haddan
iii. *Lyle Spencer Finch* m. Caren Lynette Burst

JAMES PHILLIP PIKE, b. 10 April 1936 Leavenworth; bapt. 27 September 1936, Leavenworth; only record of him was from his baptismal record, St. Joseph's Church, Leavenworth; d. 30 December 1936 of pneumonia at 6 months of age, Onaga, Kansas; buried St. Patrick's cemetery at the foot of Hugo Gustaf Holmgren, who had died on 3 October 1940. Hugo was a Navy Coxswain who was listed as James' foster father.

ROBERT EMMET PIKE AND MAMIE KATHERINE BODENSCHATZ

MARGARET JOSEPHINE PIKE, b. 15 November 1921, Leavenworth, named after her grandmother; spent her childhood in Leavenworth but then traveled to California to visit her grandmother, Pauline Bodenshatz, aunts and cousins; m1 Amos Pierrot (divorced); returned to Leavenworth and m2 David Ezell, who was stationed at the Fort; m3 Captain Robert R. Tyner in Georgia and they traveled extensively due to his career, d. 1968; worked for U.S. Government in Colorado Springs, Colorado; m4

Frank Kauffman (later divorced); transferred to Fort Hood, Texas where worked until retirement in 1992; moved to Hailey, Idaho in 1993 to be with her children; d. 26 May 2004, Boise, Idaho; cremated and spread over head lakes of Salmon River in Idaho.

Margaret and David Ezell:

i. *Carolyn Sue Ezell*
ii. *Robert Brock Ezell*
iii. *David Hartwell Ezell*
iv. *Edward Windell Ezell*

LEO CLEMENT PIKE SR. AND FRANCES MARY HECKMAN

LEO CLEMENT "BUD" PIKE JR., b. 1925 Fort Leavenworth, Kansas; graduated 1942; USArmy from 1949-, retired from Fort Campbell, Kentucky.

i. *Leo Edward Pike*

MARY MARGARET PIKE, b. 1923 Fort Leavenworth, Kansas; graduated 1940; m. Harvey C. Chadbourne; Harvey b. 17 November 1921, St. Joseph, Montana; Harvey served World War II, USAF, Retired Lt. Col from 315th Bomb Wing, interviewed by his grandson, Matthew S. Berger regarding his military career. http://lcweb2.loc.gov/cocoon/vhp/story/loc.natlib.afc2001001.04229/

transcript?ID=sr0001, Veteran's History Project.

i. *Cheryl Chadbourne*
ii. *Harvey L. Chadbourne*
iii. *Connie Chadbourne*
iv. *Cynthia Chadbourne*

MARGARET PIKE AND JOHN WILLIAM BECKER

ANNA EILEEN "EILEEN" BECKER, b. 3 March 1917, Leavenworth; a jitterbug for Leavenworth where she once danced for a group; m1 Hundsacker (spelling?) after 2 December 1934 (Pike baptismal showed Eileen's maiden name, as a witness). She only had one child, Norman Clifton. The father's whereabouts are unknown; m2 William "Bill" Gregory Schulte, 3 July 1943, Leavenworth. Bill served in the military from March 1941 to October 1946; stationed at Fort Dawson (?), Alaska (according to their bible) where he built the highways, and Camp McCoy, Wisconsin; Once he returned, he married Eileen. They had no children but Norman adopted the Schulte name; he, Eileen and Norman then moved to Iowa where Bill bought his parent's farm as he worked as a farmer for twenty years; employed by Henderson's where he hauled milk; member of the American Legion Post 45 and VFW Post 6637; he d. 20 November 1996, Manchester, Delaware County, Iowa; buried St. Boniface Cemetery, New Vienna, Iowa with full military honors; the United States flag was flown over the United States Capitol on 3 July 1988 at the request of Honorable Bob Dole, U.S. Senator and then presented by Margaret Baskas and Barbara Marsden; also presented with a certificate of military service by President William Jefferson Clinton; When Bill died, Eileen then moved back to Leavenworth and lived at the Planter's Apartments until her death on 5 July 2002; buried at Mt. Calvary, next to her mother.

Eileen and Hundsacker:

i. *Norman Clifton Hunsacker* m1. Margaret Mary Biederman; m2. Catherine Ann Pillarelli

LILLIAN MAE "LILLY MAE" BECKER, b. 20 May 1919, Leavenworth; m. Lee E. Hattok Sr., 16 July; lived in Lansing before Lee's mother died; then moved to her farm in Leavenworth where they lived; d. 1 February 1988, Leavenworth; buried Mt. Calvary, Lansing, Kansas.

i. *Lee E. Hattok*
ii. *Francis William Hattok* m. Sandra Beth Moorehead

iii. *Donna Jean Hattok* m1. Bob Wood; m2. Jesus Riog
iv. *Maxine Mae Hattok* m. Robert W. Tucker
v. *Dorothy Ann Hattok* m. Jack Messer

MARGARET PIKE (M2)
JOHN BURKE BASKAS

(see Baskas tree)

MARGARET PIKE AND
JEROME HARRISON "ROME"
WOLFE

(see Baskas tree)

CATHERINE BARRY AND
MORRIS/MAURICE ALIFF

MARY CATHERINE ALIFF, (513-16-3632) b. 13 August 1923, Kansas; m. Swartz; d. 4 August 2004 Kansas City, Kansas; funeral at St. Paul's Episcopal Church; buried Chapel Hill Memorial Gardens.

MARGARET ELIZABETH BARRY AND
HENRY PICKERING

WILLIAM E. PICKERING SR., b. 20 November 1905 by Dr. W. R. Van Tuyl, parents were living at 527 Dakota, Leavenworth; commercial car salesman; m. Josephine B.; moved to Kansas City, Missouri in 1913; member of St. John the Evangelist Catholic Church, Holy Name Society, Bishop Miege Council and Knights of Columbus; retired 1964 from Kansas City, Kansas Police Department as lieutenant; d. September 1972 Kansas City, Missouri; both buried Mt. Calvary, Kansas City, Kansas. Josephine B. b. 1907 Kansas City; bookkeeper in stationary supply; d. 23 March 1988 Charlotte; retired as machine operator for Armour & Co; burial Mt. Calvary, Kansas City, Kansas.

i.   *William E. Pickering Jr.*

RUTH T. PICKERING, b. 9 March 1907 by Dr. C. D. Lloyd, Leavenworth, parents were living at 527 Dakota; m. Raymond West about 1929, lived down the street from their parents in 1930.

AGNES C. PICKERING, b. 2 March 1910 by Dr. C. K. Vaugh, parents were living at 113 Pawnee, Leavenworth; packer in a candy factory; m. Ray G. Duffy, Kansas City, Kansas.

JAMES HENRY BARRY JR. AND FLORENCE HAMBLIN

JAMES P. BARRY, b. 1 February 1918 Leavenworth, Kansas; m. Peggy, Effingham, Kansas; d. 12 August 2005, San Mateo, California.

i.   *James Raymond Barry*
ii. *Carl G. Barry*
iii. *Carleen Marie Barry*

HOWARD FREDERICK BARRY, b. 4 August 1922 Leavenworth, Kansas; m. Mary Magdalen Heitlinger (sister to Tudy Baskas, wife of Robert Baskas); Mary d. 15 September 2008 Atchinson, Kansas; ran Barry Tavern with his father whom he lived with; World War II USA; member of American Legion and Veterans of Foreign Wars and a bartender; d. 14 July 1976, home Leavenworth; buried Mt. Calvary.

i.   *Michael G. Barry*
ii. *Colleen Barry* m. Michael J. Waite
iii. *Kathleen M. Barry* m. Knowles

CHAPTER VIII

GENERATION 3

Researcher
Richard S. Baskas

WALTER WILLIAM BASKAS AND
LOIS HUBBARD

"SCOOTER" BASKAS, d. about 2 years old of TB; **burial unknown**.

HELEN GLYNN AND
GEORGE MEEKER

MARIE ELYNOR MEEKER, b. 28 March 1924 Syracuse, New York; attended Sacred Heart Grade School, Leavenworth; Westport High, Kansas City, Missouri, 1941; R.N., St. John's Hospital School of Nursing, Leavenworth, 1944; B.S., NSG. Ed, St. Mary's College, Leavenworth, 1950; M.S., NSG. Ed, Marquette University, Milwaukee, Wisconsin, 1951; entered sisterhood 19 August 1955 as Sister Jean Patrick Meeker; took first vows, 22 August 1957; Mission, St. Vincent Hospital, Billings, Montana, 1957-60; Mission, Providence Hospital, Kansas City, Kansas, 1960-3; end of first semester, St. Mary College, Xavier, 1963; final vows, 22 August 1963; Instructor, St. Mary College, Leavenworth, 1964; Studying in Brighton, Massachusetts, Summer, 1969; M.S., Psychology, Kansas State Teacher's College, Emporia, Kansas, 1971; taught in Kansas City Institute for Women program sponsored while living in Berchman's Hall, 1973-6; Psychology Instructor, St. Mary

College, 1974-5; study leave, summer 1978; Clinical Pastoral Education (CPE) Program, Presbyterian Hospital, Denver, Colorado—student, lived at St. Joseph Hospital, Denver, 15 August 1979; departed 16 April 1980; served in U.S. Army Nurse Corp during World War II; worked in nursing administration at Veterans Affairs Hospital in Cheyenne and Reno, Nevada, Cheyenne, Wyoming as Sister Jaye P. Cassidy; d. 20 November 1999 Cheyenne, Wyoming; services held by Rev. James Doudican; cremation at Cheyenne Memorial Gardens by Wiederspahn-Radomsky Chapel of the Chimes.

ROBERT E. MEEKER, b. 1926 Leavenworth, Kansas; m. Pat E. (b. 1923); d. before 20 November 1999 (her sister's obituary).

i. *Mary Meeker*
ii. *Robert Meeker*
iii. *Nancy Meeker* m. Daniel Montgomery

PATRICIA M. MEEKER, b. 1927 Leavenworth, Kansas; m. Cecil Grimm Mauld.

i. *Pamela Mauld* m. Mark Strayhorn
ii. *Patrick J. Mauld* m. Cynthia
iii. *Cynthia Mauld* m. Delmas Virgil Linhart Jr.

iv. *Cindy Mauld*
v. *Lisa Mauld*

BLANCHE C. GLYNN AND JOHN D. BECHER

BLANCHE M. BECHER, b. 1926 Leavenworth, Kansas; St. Mary's Academy, 1944 and 1948; m. Raymond Joseph Lippman Sr.

i. *Raymond Joseph "Skip" Lippman*
ii. *Mary Patricia Lippman* m. Mahon
iii. *Ann Louise Lippman*
iv. *John Kevin Lippman*
v. *Paula M. Lippman*

JOSEPH LAWRENCE "BOOTS" GLYNN SR. AND ALICE L.

JEAN ELLEN (JOANNE?) GLYNN, m. Harris

WILLIAM GLYNN, Navy, USS Taylor, Hull #DD-468, E-5, August 1963-July 1968, Tin Can Sailors.

JEROME GLYNN.

Ronald Glynn

BARBARA GLYNN, m. Packard, Sacramento, California.

JOSEPH LAWRENCE GLYNN JR., b. August 1932 Mobile, Alabama; B.S., Finance, 1967 ('63-'67), University of Portland, Oregon; m. Jacquelyn, nurse; d. 23 October 1972 Multnomah, Oregon; buried Gethsemani Cemetery, Oregon.

i. *Margaret J. Glynn*
ii. *Karen E. Glynn*
iii. *Laura C. Glynn*

JOHN WALTER GLYNN SR. AND DOROTHY ALICE MARTIN

JOHN WALTER GLYNN JR., b. 23 August 1940 Leavenworth, Kansas; m. Barbara Anne Bachmann; Barbara, B.A. History, Trinity College, Washington; M.A. History, University of Virginia; current founder of the Tech Museum of Innovation in San Jose, California; serves on board of several schools and community agencies including Family Service Organization; B.A., History, University Notre Dame, 1962; LLB (Bachelor of Law), University of Virginia School of Law, 1965 then worked for McCutchen, Doyle, Brown & Enersen in San Francisco; left firm and attended and earned MBA, Graduate School of Business, Stanford University, 1970 then worked for venture capital firm. In 1974, started his own venture capital business. Since 1990 taught venture capital courses to second-year MBA students at Darden Graduate School of Business at University of Virginia and Stanford Graduate School of Business. Founder and president of Glynn Capital Management LLC (Limited Liability Company-type of business that offers an alternative to partnerships and corporations, by combining the corporate advantages of limited liability with the partnership advantage of pass-through taxation where earnings are taxed only once), since 1983; Visiting Lecturer, Darden School, University of Virginia, 1990-2004; Visiting Lecturer, Cambridge University, 1999-2004; established The Glynn Family Scholarship (in 1996, with his daughter, Alexandra): awarded every year to a rising junior who is an economics major and when possible, to any student who has shown an interest in an entrepreneurial business career and community service. Affiliations—Advisory Board: Judge Institute of Management, Cambridge University Graduate School of Business and College of Arts and Letters at University of Notre Dame; Director: Several private companies; Member: California State Bar Assn., Catilleja School Finance Committee; Past President: Stanford GSB Alumni Assn., San Francisco Chapter and

Trustee: University of Virginia School of Law.

i.   *Alexandra Donovan Glynn* m. David Newton Rowe
ii. *Jacqueline Martin Glynn* m. Patrick Eck Brandin
iii. *David Glynn*
iv. *Elizabeth Charles Glynn*

LINDA SUE GLYNN, b. 9 April 1944 Leavenworth, Kansas; University of Mary Washington, Fredericksburg, Virginia, class of 1966; m. David William Hutchinson 16 May 1970 Hampton, Virginia.

i.   *Shannon Glynn Hutchinson* m. Nicholas Lee Crockett
ii. *Morgan Suzanne Hutchinson* m. Brian James Gosey
iii. *David Martin Hutchinson*

JOHN JOSEPH "BUDDY" BASKAS AND MARY MARGARET CROOK

PAMELA ANN BASKAS, b. 5 February 1946 Leavenworth; d. 14 September 1990; worked as a buyer and sales clerk for Bohm's Department Store; m. Ronald E. Jones, 20 November 1965; buried Mt. Calvary.

i.   *Christopher Allen Jones*
ii. *Sandra K. Jones* m. Jones

ANGELA MARIE BASKAS, b. 24 November 1946 Leavenworth;

m. Eugene Everett Hacker, 4 July 1966; Eugene, b. 24 November 1946 Salt Lake City, Utah, d. 27 November 2001 Leavenworth. He served in USN, worked as senior lab technician for Hallmark Card Company, was an avid fisherman and antique collector, buried Mt. Calvary.

i.   *Robert John Hacker* m. Janine Shopbell
ii. *Danielle Rene Hacker* m1. Andrews, m2. Trautman

KATHY LEE BASKAS, b. 13 February 1953 Leavenworth; IMAC, '71; m. Mike Goldak, 7 June 1975; accountant at Penitentiary and retired 2003;

i.   *Patrick Michael Goldak*
ii. *Ellen Ann Goldak*

JOHN "SKIP" JOSEPH BASKAS JR., b. 15 September 1956 Leavenworth; Leavenworth High '74; m. Sharon Fevurly, 26 September 1974.

i.   *Christine Baskas* m. Jason Randall
ii. *John James Baskas*

LEO DANIEL "BLACKIE" BASKAS AND MILDRED OVERMAN

LEO DANIEL "DANNY" BASKAS JR., b. 17 August 1949 Leavenworth; Army; m. Yolanda Louise Martinez.

i.   *Lea Marie Baskas* m. Reynaldo Trejo Jr.
ii. *Daniel Eric Baskas*

RITA MARIE "KITTY" BASKAS, b. 28 August 1950 Leavenworth; m. Charles Albro Stine III 13 October 1969 Los Vegas, Nevada.

i.   *Charles Albro Stine IV*
ii. *Candice Amber Stine* m. Jones

WILLIAM ANTHONY BASKAS, b. 10 March 1957 Leavenworth; Leavenworth High, '74; m. Joan Reed 22 August 1995.

FRANK WILLIAM BASKAS AND LOUETTA KATHERINE KENNY

TERRI LOU BASKAS, (adopted), b. 27 February 1958 Orange County, California; m1 Mike Bielka; m2 McManms; m3 Teavebaugh; d. 2008.

i.   *Manda Lynn Bielka* m. Clark
ii. *Tiffany Teavebaugh*
iii. *Jacob Dale Teavebaugh*

TOM EMMETT BASKAS AND WILDA JUNE SNIDER

LINDA KAY BASKAS, b. 20 September 1955; m. Tim J. Berger 3 August 1975, Peoria, Illinois; attended Immaculate Conception in first grade; she and her parents moved to Peoria in 1962; graduated from St. John's in 8th grade; graduated from Manual High School, 1974; attended Bradley University (non-degree) with classes in Business Management; works for Key Industry in East Peoria as assistant supervisor of 3 departments, manufacturing, shipping and engraving.

i.   *Nicholas Aaron Thomas Berger*
ii. *Ashlyn Taylor Berger*

ROBERT EDWARD BASKAS AND VIVIAN ROSE "TUDY" HEITLINGER

VIVIAN LEE BASKAS, b. 13 October 1948; m. Robert Tracey Berg Sr.

i.   *Robert Tracey Berg* m. Amy Elizabeth
ii. *Shari Leigh Berg* m. Randall Kent Herder

SHARON LOUISE BASKAS, b. 2 December 1951; IMAC, '70; m. Clarence "Clancy" Albert Filbert, 8 April 1972; d. 17 October 2002 Weston, Missouri.

i.   *Cassandra "Cassy" Lynn Filbert* m1. Randall Eugene Bradford; m2. J. Pennington
ii. *Katherine Renee Filbert* m. Scott Ray Watkins

RALPH VINCENT "PORKY" BASKAS
AND JOANN SHASICK

MICHELLE RENEE BASKAS, b. 5 October 1964 Leavenworth; m. Thomas Benjamin Portenier Jr. 13 February 1982 Platte City, Missouri, d. 21 September 2003 Lawrence Missouri of a boating accident.

i.   *Rachel Renee Portenier* m. M. Berg
ii. *Stacey Michelle Portenier* m. Watkins
iii. *Thomas Benjamin Portenier*

MICHAEL CHARLES BASKAS SR. AND
UNA MAE SHASICK

KIMBERLY LYNN BASKAS, b. 24 October 1967 Leavenworth

MICHAEL CHARLES BASKAS JR., b. 16 January 1973 Leavenworth; m1 Julie L. Hartman 15 January 1999 Clark County, Nevada; m2 Jamie Sotomayor, Leavenworth High, 1993.

Michael and Jamie:

i.   *Andrew Trinidad Eugene Baskas*

JAMES ANTHONY "JIM" BASKAS
AND BETTY EMMA KARNES

RICHARD   SCOTT   "SCOTT" BASKAS, b. 8 April 1965 Merced, California; Clinton, MD: Crestview Elementary; Surrattsville Jr. and Sr. High; Forestville: Bishop McNamara; LaPlata, MD: Charles County Community College, *AA, General Studies*; Salisbury, MD: Salisbury State University, *BS, Biology*.

Military: USAF (8 April 1992-30 April 2004)
Basic Training: Lackland AFB, Texas; Tech School: Fire School, Chanute AFB, Illinois; 1st Base: Langley AFB, VA; 2nd Base: Soto Cano AB, Honduras; 3rd Base: MacDill AFB, FL; 1st TDY: Al Dafra AB, Saudi Arabia; 2nd TDY: Columbia, South America; 3rd TDY: Eskan Village, Saudi Arabia; Langley AFB, VA: Community College of the Air Force, *A.A.S., Fire Science*; *Airman Leadership School*

Awards and Medals

Air Force Achievement Medal
Joint Meritorious Unit Award
Outstanding Unit Award
Organization Excellence Award
Good Conduct Medal
National Defense Service Medal
Air Expeditionary Group Medal

Southwest Asia Campaign
Humanitarian Service Medal
Overseas Short Tour
Longevity Service Award
NCO Prof. Military Education
Graduate
Air Force Training

Author:

Baskas, R. (2007). *My Family History: Pioneers of Custer County, Montana and Leavenworth, Kansas: Descendants of Kanelly, Barry, Roache, Pike, Baskas and McMahon.* Xlibris Pub. Co., Philadelphia, PA.

Baskas, R. (2008) *Cornelius Melyn: 3ʳᵈ Patroon of Staten Island, New York, His Children and Some Descendants.* Xlibris Pub. Co., Philadelphia, PA.

Master of Arts in Teaching (M.A.T.): *Science Education*, University of South Florida, Tampa (Spring 2010); passed all parts of FCTE to become certified as secondary school teacher.

JAMES ALLEN BASKAS, b. 8 May 1967 Leavenworth, Kansas; bapt. 29 May 1967 IMAC by Rev. L. F. Horner with sponsors Juanita and Elis Rodriguez. He grew up in Clinton, Maryland with his brother where he went to school; Crestview Elementary, Clinton, 1980; St. Mary's Grade School, Piscataway,

1982; Surrattsville Jr. and Sr., Clinton, 1983-6 while attending Gwynn Park High for his trade in Air Conditioning and Refrigeration and Lincoln Tech School, MD; moved with his parents and brother to Florida in 1990 where he shared a place with his brother for a few years. His brother joined the USAF and James later got his own home; worked for Del-Air in Lake Mary, Florida from 1990 until his death, 23 Apr 2003; cremated in Deltona; buried Mt. Calvary Cemetery with Gma Baskas, Lansing, Kansas on 14 June 2003. Fr. David McEvoy said the ceremony at the cemetery and mass at St. Joseph's in Leavenworth

MARGARET KATHERINE CANTWELL
AND CHARLES JOSEPH ARNOLD

MARY MARGARET ARNOLD, b. 19 December 1924, El Paso, Texas; bapt. St. Joseph's with George L. Arnold and Katherine Briesh as witnesses; m. Michael J. Devlin Jr., 27 November 1947, St. Patrick's at 9 am mass by Rev. Buckley. Attendants were Tommy Devlin, Charlotte Arnold as Best Man; Bernice Arnold, Geraldine Brown Wheelock and Sammie Brosnahan as Brides Maids; and Bill Johnstone and Lee Floyd as Ushers.

i.   *Colleen Elizabeth Devlin*

ii.   *Michael Joseph Devlin III*
iii. *Dennis Arnold Devlin*
iv.   *Patrick Lee Devlin*

CHARLOTTE JOSEPHINE ARNOLD, b. 9 March 1927, El Paso, Texas; bapt. St. Joseph's with P.L. Cantwell and Mary Geraldine Brown; m. William Lee Sitton, 10 June 1950, St. Patrick's during 10 am mass by Rev. Vander Harr. Reception was at 1215 Rim Road, Kay Briesh's house; Bernice Arnold as Maid of Honor; Fred Sitton as Best man and Betty Jago and Geraldine Wheelock as Brides Maids.

i.   *Beverly Ann Sitton*
ii.   *Susan Maria Sitton*
iii. *Patrick Leigh Sitton*
iv.   *Thomas Fitzhugh Sitton*

BERNICE TERESA ARNOLD, b. 3 May 1930; bapt. St. Patrick's with F.J. Cantwell and Mary G. Brown as sponsors; m1 Jack Ekey, October 1951; m2 Charles Elwin Haskins, 1 June 1955, d. 31 December 1999 El Paso, buried Ft. Bliss, WW II.

i.   *Katheryn Ann Haskins m. Potts*
ii.   *William Roger Haskins*
iii. *Delmar C. Haskins*

FRANCIS JOSEPH CANTWELL AND MADELINE SEIBERT

JOHN ANTHONY CANTWELL, b. 18 December 1938, El Paso; bapt. Holy Family Church by Rev. Burkley with C. J. Arnold and Betty Seibert as sponsors; d. 24 January 1992, Albuquerque, New Mexico

ELLEN CANTWELL, b. 11 July 1942

KENNETH CANTWELL, b. 28 September 1943

ANN CANTWELL, b. 13 December 1944.

MARY GERALDINE CANTWELL AND LEONARD WILSON BROWN

GERALDINE PATRICIA BROWN, b. 7 August 1926, El Paso; bapt. St. Patrick's with P.L. Cantwell and Margaret Arnold as witnesses; m. Richard Chester Wheelock, 15 March 1947, Post Chapel, Fort Bliss, Texas by Rev. (Lt. Col.?) Connally, Mary Margaret Arnold as Maid of Honor; Charlotte Arnold, Margori Sanders and Martha Kilpatrick as Brides Maids; Ellen Cantwell as flower girl; and Wilson Durr as Best Man; reception at 1430 Hawthorne.

i.   *Catherine Lee Wheelock*

KATHERINE MARIE MOTTIN AND HUGO BRIESH

PAUL BRIESH

MARY KATHERINE (MARY KAY) BRIESH

HELEN ROSE MOTTIN AND EARL FRANCIS BROSNAHAN SR.

HELEN DESALME (SAMMIE) BROSNAHAN, b. 4 January 1926 Kansas City, Missouri; bapt. 18 January 1926 St. Joseph's, Lowemont, Kansas, sponsored by Leger and Catharine Mottin; St. Mary's Academy '43; St. Mary's College; University of Arizona; and BA, English, University of Texas, El Paso; m1 Lewis Johnston Vaughan, 29 March 1948, St. Peters, Kansas City, Missouri; m2 John Boren Criswell, 22 April 1974 St. Mathew's Church, El Paso, Texas; retired after 30 years as an elementary school counselor and teacher. Her years at St. Mary's were "memorable, memorable years; I loved it." She reflected on her mother turned 100, "As an elementary school counselor I realized how important one's parents are, and I was very fortunate; the chair that "Munnie"is sitting is where Sammie sat during which she interviewed her grandmother for the folklore paper she wrote for school for which part of it was used in this tree.

i. *Mary Helen Vaughan* m. Charles Wayne Flora

KATHERINE MOTTIN BROSNAHAN, b. 12 June 1927; d. 24 April 1934

EARL FRANCIS "FRANK" BROSNAHAN JR., b. 31 July 1928, Kansas City, Missouri; m1 June Therese Mullen, 18 April 1953; m2 Kathryn Maureen 'Sandy' Palmer.

Earl and June:

i. *Michelle Theresa Brosnahan* m. Jon Reese Pozgay
ii. *Earl Francis Brosnahan III* m. Carol Best
iii. *Anne Mullen Brosnahan* m1. Steven Burstein; m2. Nicholas Lee DiVita
iv. *Reta Mottin Brosnahan* m. Karl Saffo
v. *Katherine Noel "Kate" Brosnahan* m. Andrew Spade
vi. *Eve Mullen Brosnahan*

(DR.) LEGER NICHOLAS MOTTIN "LEGE" BROSNAHAN SR., b. 11 December 1929, Kansas City, Missouri; Rockchurst Prep School in Kansas City, Missouri; AB, Georgetown '51; MA, Harvard '52; PhD, English, Harvard '58; m. (Dr.) Irene Mayshir "Matz" Teoh, 2 November 1967, Toronto, Canada,

English Professor, b. 24 June 1937 Gulangyu, Xiamin, China; AB, Hong Kong University '59; MA, University of Hawaii '63; PhD, Georgetown '72; Professor Emerita of English, Illinois State University, teaches Linguistics and TESOL until retired in June 2004; involved in Illinois TESOL/BE for many years, served various capacities on Executive Board-Parliamentarian, First Vice President, President, Past President and for two years, Editor of ITBE Newsletter.

i. *Leger Nicholas Bronahan Jr.* m. Anna Margarete Jaeckel
ii. *Jennifer Ru-Chiao Brosnahan* m. Kevin Joseph McIntyre

MARY VIRGINIA "GINNY" BROSNAHAN, b. 20 January 1933 Kansas City, Missouri; B.A., Kansas University; m. Dr. Benjamin D. McCallister, b. 24 July 1932 Fort Worth, Texas; Cardiovascular Surgeon and Consultant, Vice chair and on Board of Mid-American Heart Institute, Kansas City, Missouri; Professor of Medicine at University of Missouri-Kansas City School of Medicine; On boards of Midwest Research Institute and St. Luke's Hospital Foundation; B.A. and M.D. from University of Kansas; U.S. Army, Captain, Medical Corps, 1957-61; initial career at Mayo Clinic 1961-9; completed Fellowship in

cardiology; National Institutes of Health Research Fellow.

i. *(Dr.) Benjamin D. McCallister Jr.* m. Elizabeth Meeker
ii. *(Dr.) Scott Horton McCallister* m. Julie
iii. *John Gregory McCallister* m. Caroline Lee Price Rhoden
iv. *Thomas Mottin McCallister* m. Gail McClelland Davis
v. *Katherine Ann McCallister* m. Joseph Louis Cubba

ROGER PAUL "ROG" BROSNAHAN, b. 9 August 1935 Kansas City, Missouri; 1980-1 Past President of NCBP (Nat. Conf. Bar Pres.), Wisconsin; m. Jill Ann Farley.

i. *Paul Farley Brosnahan* m. Jan Mackenzie Peterson
ii. *Connor Francis Brosnahan* m. Judith K. Ha
iii. *Tracey Turner Vivian Brosnahan* m2. Mitchell John Lobin
iv. *Peter Farley Brosnahan*
v. *Helen Rose Mottin Brosnahan* m. Michael Steven Zauha
vi. *Lee Patrick Brosnahan* m. Christina Caroline Young
vii. *Hugh Bihm Brosnahan* m1?; m2. Jennifer

JOHN JOSEPH BROSNAHAN, b. 19 March 1944 Kansas City, Missouri; lawyer; m. Marilyn Puiung Chow (b. 1947) 16 December 1984 San

Francisco, California. They had no children.

GRACE ISADORA MOTTIN AND GERALD SAMUEL O'BRENNAN

BRIAN LEGER O'BRENNAN, d. 1984

GERALD ALAN O'BRENNAN, d. 2004

MARY ANDREA O'BRENNAN, m. Mark Moulton, d. 1999.

ROSEMARY O'BRENNAN, m. Wade Bailey Parks

i. *Dustin Wade Parks*
ii. *Chris Parks*
iii. *Chase Brian Parks*

ROBERT LeROY PIKE AND CHARLENE GABRIC

CONSTANCE "CONNIE" JEAN PIKE

ROBERT LE ROY PIKE AND DORCILLE PHILLIPS

ROBERTA "BOBBIE" KATHLEEN PIKE, b. 29 September 1953, Atchison, Kansas; m1. Berry; m2. Charley Shoemaker.

i. *Patrick Timothy Berry*
ii. *Michael Sean Berry*

THOMAS CLIFFORD "PICK" PIKE AND EVELYN L. PAYNE

ROBERT LEE PIKE, b. 15 June 1957 Leavenworth, Kansas; Army; Leavenworth firefighter 1985-90 retired; m. Lisa A.

i. *Kathleen L. Pike*
ii. *Kevin R. Pike*

JANET PIKE, m. Carter.

i. *Chuck Carter*
ii. *Amanda Carter*
iii. *Cassie Carter* m. Josh Jones

MARGARET "PEGGY" JANE PIKE (BARKER) AND FELIX CORDOVA

DENNIE RAE CORDOVA (BARKER), m. Nancy

i. *Shawn Barker*

MARGARET "PEGGY" JANE PIKE (BARKER) AND SPENCER LEE FINCH

PAUL SAMUEL FINCH, b. 26 November 1956, Florence, Colorado; Air Force Cop; m. (later divorced) Nancy Lyn Haddan, Black Forest, Colorado

i. *David Spencer Finch*
ii. *Michael Paul Finch*

LYLE SPENCER FINCH, b. 3 February 1964, Colorado Springs, Colorado; m. Caren Lynette Burst, 22 December 1984, Colorado Springs, Colorado.

i.   *Adam Charles Finch*
ii. *Elias Kane Finch*

MARGARET JOSEPHINE PIKE AND DAVID EZELL

CAROLYN SUE EZELL

ROBERT BROCK EZELL

DAVID HARTWELL EZELL

EDWARD WINDELL EZELL

LEO CLEMENT "BUD" PIKE JR.

Leo Edward Pike

MARY MARGARET PIKE AND HARVEY C. CHADBOURNE

Cheryl Chadbourne

Harvey L. Chadbourne

Connie Chadbourne

Cynthia Chadbourne

ANNA EILEEN BECKER AND HUNDSACKER

NORMAN CLIFTON HUNDSACKER, b. 9 March 1941, Leavenworth, Kansas; served Navy at NAS, Key West for one year; m1 Margaret Mary Biederman, 30 January 1960, Coggon, Iowa; m2 Catherine Ann Pillarelli; d. 15 December 1992, Scottsdale, Arizona; cremated and buried Mt. Calvary, next to his grandmother, Margaret Pike-Baskas.

Norman and Margaret:

i.   *Rex Robert Schulte* m1. Bobbie Whitney; m3. Donna Petrie
ii. *Robin Renee Schulte* m1. Randy L. Berry
iii. *Rhett Randall Schulte* m1. Ann
iv. *Rhonda Rae Schulte* m1. Steven Richard Sr.
v.   *Rhafe Random Schulte*

Norman and Catherine:

vi. *Michael Clifton Schulte*

LILLIAN MAE BECKER AND LEE HATTOK SR.

LEE E. HATTOK

i.   *Paul J. Hattok*
ii. *Brian Hattok*
iii. *Nancy Hattok*

iv.   *John Hattok*

v.   *Lee Hattok Jr.* m. Ann

FRANCIS WILLIAM HATTOK, b. 21 September 1941; m. Sandra Beth Moorehead 16 July 1966, Leavenworth; USArmy, Fort Leonard Wood, Missouri.

i.   *John F. Hattok*

DONNA JEAN HATTOK, m1 Bob Wood; m2 Jesus Riog

i.   *Connie Wood*

ii.   *Debbie Wood*

iii.   *Renee Riog*

MAXINE MAE HATTOK, b. 18 February 1946; m. Robert W. Tucker

i.   *Ronnie Tucker*

ii.   *Rebecca Tucker*

iii.   *Richard Tucker*

iv.   *Misty Tucker*

v.   *Robert Tucker*

DOROTHY ANN HATTOK, m. Jack Messer.

i.   *Jeremy Messer*

WILLIAM E. PICKERING SR. AND JOSEPHINE B.

WILLIAM E. PICKERING JR., lived in Roanoke, Virginia by 1972.

JAMES P. BARRY AND PEGGY

JAMES RAYMOND BARRY, b. 1952

CARL G. BARRY (Fraternal twin), b. 29 October 1957 San Mateo, California

CARLEEN MARIE BARRY (Fraternal twin), b. 29 October 1957 San Mateo, California

i.   *James P. Barry*

ii.   *Margaret C. Barry*

iii.   *Sheldon C. Barry*

iv.   *Donielle Elizabeth Barry*

HOWARD FREDERICK BARRY AND MARY MAGDALINE HEITLINGER

MICHAEL G. BARRY

COLLEEN BARRY, b. 27 January 1953; m. Michael J. Waite, 28 May 1977 Fort Leavenworth; he d. 3 February 2008, University of Kansas Hospital. Michael graduated from Kansas University with a Bachelor's degree in 1975. He was awarded his Juris Doctor degree from Washburn University School of Law in 1978. He was engaged in the private practice of law in Leavenworth following admission to the bar for 29 years. During his 29 years of practice he concentrated on criminal defense, appearing regularly before the District Courts of the State of Kansas as well as presenting cases before the Kansas Court of Appeals, the Kansas Supreme Court and The United States Court of Appeals for the Tenth Circuit. Michael retired from private practice due to deteriorating health in 2007; past member of the, Kansas Bar Association (KBA); The Leavenworth County Bar Association; The Kansas Trial Lawyers Association (KTLA); and the Kansas Association of Criminal Defense Attorneys (KACDA); member of the local contract panel of attorneys, appointed by Kansas District Court Judges to represent indigent criminal defendants charged with misdemeanors as well as minors charged with juvenile offenses and children who were found to be children in need of care. He represented adults charged with more serious felony offenses in state courts. He also was a court appointed defense attorney for Leavenworth Municipal Court for the past 10 years. Michael was a key force in forming the Annual Leavenworth County Bar Association Golf Tournament. He was instrumental in establishing the tradition of giving the proceeds of this event to local charities. His efforts helped to produce a regular annual contribution to the local charities selected by the Leavenworth County Bar Association. The total financial contribution his efforts produced is incalculable. His participation will be missed by the members of the Bar Association and the charities his efforts assisted. He was the unofficial "Welcoming Committee" to new members of the Leavenworth Bar. Michael would take time to greet and welcome all new attorneys and would introduce them to other older more experienced members. He was kind, not only in court, but also warm and charming at social occasions. Michael was an outstanding member of the Bar in his personal interactions with those who needed his counsel and insight; buried, cremated.

i.   *Zachary Waite*

KATHLEEN M. BARRY, m. Knowles

CHAPTER IX

GENERATIONS 4 & 5

Researcher
Richard S. Baskas

ROBERT E. MEEKER AND PAT E.

MARY MEEKER

ROBERT MEEKER

NANCY MEEKER, m. Daniel Montgomery

PATRICK J. MAULD, b. 1 September 1961; m. Cynthia

CYNTHIA N. MAULD, b. 1 September 1962; m. Delmas Virgil Linhart Jr.

CINDY MAULD

LISA G. MAULD, b. 1964

PATRICIA M. MEEKER AND CECIL GRIMM MAULD

PAMELA MAULD, m. Mark Strayhorn.

i.   *Travis Strayhorn*
ii. *Brice Strayhorn*

BLANCHE M. BECHER AND RAYMOND JOSEPH LIPPMAN SR.

RAYMOND "SKIP" JOSEPH LIPPMAN JR., b. 13 November 1947; attended college; adopted 3 and had one of own.

i.   *Joe Lippman*

ii. *Roberta Victoria Lippman (adopted)*

iii. *Matthew Jason Lippman (adopted)*

MARY PATRICIA LIPPMAN, b. 19 April 1949; m. Mahon, Army Col.; lived in D.C.; attended Walter Reed Nursing School, Maryland; Kansas University; Maryland University; Director of Nursing, Pentagon; has 2 kids; lives in Aptose, CA

ANN LOUISE LIPPMAN, b. 1 December 1953 Detroit, Michigan; d. 21 September 1962 Kansas City, Kansas; buried Mt. Calvary.

JOHN KEVIN LIPPMAN, b. 8 January 1958; Pharmaceuticals, Philadelphia, not married

PAULA M. LIPPMAN, b. 14 January 1964; worked at Pizza Hut as hostess; had Apert's Syndrome (retardation); member of Association for Retarded Citizens (ARC) and served on board of directors for many years; president of ARC Self Advocates; d. 15 June 2000, Leavenworth; buried Mt. Calvary.

JOSEPH LAWRENCE GLYNN JR. AND JACQUELYN

MARGARET J. GLYNN, m. Kevin Twilleager.

KAREN ELIZABETH GLYNN

LAURA CATHERINE GLYNN, m. George Pouch

JOHN WALTER GLYNN JR. AND BARBARA ANNE BACHMANN

ALEXANDRA DONOVAN GLYNN, b. 1 September 1948; Undergraduate, 1992—3; m. David Newton Rowe.

JACQUELINE "JACKIE" MARTIN GLYNN, b. 1967 Atherton, California; B.S., History, Davidson College, Davidson, North Carolina, 1989; MBA, University of Virginia, Darden School of Business, 1993; joined Glynn Capital Management as Portfolio Investment Manager where she specializes in software and internet; analyst in investment banking department of Alex, Brown & Sons, Inc, 1989-91; m. Patrick Eck Brandin, b. 1966.

i. *Katherine Alice Brandin* b. 14 January 2003 San Francisco, California

ii. *Margaret Ann Brandin* b. 14 October 2005 San Francisco, California

DAVID SCOTT GLYNN, b. 13 December 1976 Atherton, California; B.A., English, Notre Dame, 2000.

ELIZABETH CHARLES GLYNN, b. 29 September 1983 Atherton, California; B.A., History, Notre Dame, 2006.

LINDA SUE GLYNN AND DAVID WILLIAM HUTCHINSON

SHANNON GLYNN HUTCHINSON, b. 14 November 1977 Greensburg, Pennsylvania; University of Mary Washington, Fredericksburg, Virginia; m. Nicholas Lee Crokett 22 July 2000 Washington, D.C. Temple, Kensington, Maryland; Nick, University of Mary Washington

MORGAN SUZANNE HUTCHINSON, b. 17 December 1979 Welch, West Virginia; m. Brian James Gosey 28 May 2004 St. Mary's Church, Glenshaw, Pennsylvania.

i. *Grace Logan Gosey* b. 13 October 2005 Easely, South Carolina

DAVID MARTIN HUTCHINSON, b. 10 November 1983 Pittsburgh, Pennsylvania; B.S., University of Mary Washington, Fredericksburg, Virginia, May 2006, Magna Cum Laude (Dean's List).

PAMELA ANN BASKAS AND RONALD E. JONES

CHRISTOPHER ALLEN JONES, b. 12 November 1967 Leavenworth.

i. *Kelsey Lynn Jones*, b. 12 April 1991 Leavenworth
ii. *Taylor Ann Jones*, b. 19 April 1993 Leavenworth

SANDRA K. JONES, (adopted), m. Jones.

i. *Cooper McClaine Jones*, b. 23 May 2003 Leavenworth; bapt. 8 February 2004 Sacred Heart, Leavenworth

ANGELA MARIE BASKAS AND EUGENE EVERETT HACKER

ROBERT JOHN HACKER, b. 27 December 1967 Leavenworth; m. Janine Shopbell.

i. *Gabrielle "Gabby" Hacker*, b. 17 December 1993 Leavenworth
ii. *Robert John "RJ" Hacker*, b. 27 December 1997 Leavenworth

DANIELLE RENE HACKER, b. 12 April 1973 Leavenworth; Leavenworth High, '91; m1 Andrews; m2 Trautman.

i. *Jordan Renee Andrews*, b. 25 October 1994 Leavenworth
ii. *Jesse Trautman*, b. Leavenworth

KATHY LEE BASKAS AND MIKE GOLDAK

PATRICK MICHAEL GOLDAK, b. 17 October 1988 Leavenworth; attending Kansas State University, Manhattan, KS.

ELLEN ANN GOLDAK, b. 24 January 1991 Leavenworth.

JOHN JOSEPH "SKIP" BASKAS JR. AND SHARON FEVURLY

CHRISTINE BASKAS, b. 25 August 1981 Leavenworth; m. Jason Randall.

i. *Jericho Scott Randall*, b. 22 July 2000 Leavenworth
ii. *Joshua Ezekiel Joseph Randall*, b. 9 September 2003 Leavenworth
iii. *Isaac Jacob Randall*, b. Leavenworth

JOHN JAMES BASKAS, b. 8 April 1984 Leavenworth.

LEO DANIEL "DANNY" BASKAS JR. AND YOLANDA LOUISE MARTINEZ

LEA MARIE BASKAS, b. 2 January 1977 Oxnard, California; m. Reynaldo Trejo Jr.

i. *Elizabeth Gaselle Trejo*

DANIEL ERIC BASKAS, b. 25 October 1978 Oxnard, California; served USMC, Camp Pendleton, California; Operation Iraqi Freedom (February-30 May 2003); humvee driver for company and commander (Captain Massey) and carried a weapon; in Weapons Company, which was separate from other companies; but did go to Basra, An Nasarijah and Baghdad; assisted medivacs with several injured Marines; separated for a period of time then returned; volunteered for duty in Horn of Africa (10 miles from Somalia) for Peace Keeping.

RITA MARIE "KITTY" BASKAS AND CHARLES ALBRO STINE III

CHARLES STINE IV, b. 30 July 1970

CANDICE AMBER STINE, b. 8 March 1974; m. Jones.

i. *Tyler Jones*, b. 15 June 1994

TERRI LOU BASKAS AND
MIKE BIELKA

MANDA LYNN BIELKA, b. 4 July 1977, m. Clark.

i.   *Mariah Dawn Clark*

TERRI LOU BASKAS AND
"TEAVEBAUGH"

TIFFANY TEAVEBAUGH, b. 23 February 1987

JACOB DALE TEAVEBAUGH, b. 3 December 1991.

LINDA KAY BASKAS AND
TIM J. BERGER

NICHOLAS AARON THOMAS BERGER, b. 18 February 1992

ASHLYN TAYLOR BERGER, b. 9 February 1993.

VIVIAN LEE BASKAS AND
ROBERT TRACEY BERG SR.

ROBERT TRACEY BERG JR., b. 10 April 1968; m. Amy Elizabeth1 August 1998.

i.   *Taylor Gentry Berg*, b. 1 March 1994
ii. *Ethan Berg*

SHARI LEIGH BERG, b. 27 November 1969; m. Randall Kent Herder 16 March 1991.

i.   *Brett Mitchell Herder*, b. 2 February 1994
ii. *Tess Olivia Herder*, b. 10 March 1996

SHARON LOUISE BASKAS AND
CLARENCE ALBERT FILBERT

CASSANDRA "CASSY" LYNN FILBERT, b. 11 February 1974; m1 Randall Eugene Bradford 30 December 1995; m2 J. Pennington.

i.   *Arianna Paige Bradford*, b. 16 January 1997
ii. *Maria Pennington*

KATHERINE RENEE FILBERT, b. 24 November 1975; m. Scott Ray Watkins 13 June 1997.

i.   *Darienne Marie Watkins*, b. 2 May 1997
ii. *Dalton Watkins*, b. 14 August 1999

MICHELLE RENEE BASKAS AND
THOMAS BENJAMIN PORTENIER JR.

RACHEL RENEE PORTENIER, b. 4 August 1982 Leavenworth, and "M. Berg".

i. *Makenzie Berg*, b.
    Leavenworth

STACEY MICHELLE PORTENIER,
b. 4 July 1985 Leavenworth; m.
Watkins

i. *Jackson Thomas Watkins*, b. 9
    July 2009

**THOMAS BENJAMIN PORTENIER
III**, b. 8 June 1990 Leavenworth;
Leavenworth High, 2009.

MICHAEL CHARLES BASKAS JR. AND JAMIE SOTOMAYOR

ANDREW TRINIDAD EUGENE BASKAS,
b. 9 January 2005 Kansas City,
Kansas.

MARY MARGARET ARNOLD AND MICHAEL J. DEVLIN JR.

COLLEEN ELIZABETH DEVLIN, b. 3
August 1950 El Paso, Texas; bapt.
St. Patrick's Cathedral witnessed
by Godparents, Bernice Arnold and
Tom Devlin.

MICHAEL JOSEPH DEVLIN III, b. 9
February 1952 El Paso, Texas; bapt.
St. Patrick's Cathedral, sponsored
by Lee and Alice Floyd.

DENNIS ARNOLD DEVLIN, b. 19
January 1955 Hotel Dieu Hospital;

bapt. St. Patrick's Cathedral with
sponsors Charlotte and Bill Sitton.

PATRICK LEE DEVLIN, b. 18 July 1958
El Paso, Texas; bapt. St. Patrick's
Cathedral with Godparents, Patrick
and Margaret Cantwell.

CHARLOTTE JOSEPHINE ARNOLD AND WILLIAM LEE SITTON

BEVERLY ANN SITTON, b. 28 October
1951; bapt. El Paso with Mrs. Mary
Jane Fuller and Robert Flynn as
witnesses.

SUSAN MARIA SITTON, b. 9 December
1953.

PATRICIA LEIGH SITTON, b. 1
November 1956.

THOMAS FITZHUGH SITTON, b. 23
March 1959.

BERNICE TERESA ARNOLD AND CHARLES ELWIN HASKINS

KATHERYN ANN HASKINS, b. 2
February 1956; bapt. St. Patrick's
Cathedral, El Paso, Texas with
Godparents, Charlotte and Bill
Sitton; m. Potts.

WILLIAM ROGER HASKINS, b. 12
August 1958; bapt. St. Patrick's
Cathedral, El Paso, Texas with

Godparents Mike and Mary Margaret Devlin.

DELMAR C. HASKINS

GERALDINE PATRICIA BROWN AND RICHARD CHESTER WHEELOCK

CATHERINE LEE WHEELOCK, b. 8 July 1949; bapt. 24 Jul 1949 El Paso, Texas with Ellen Flynn and Michael Devlin Jr. as sponsors.

KATHERINE MOTTIN AND HUGO BRIESH

MARY HELEN VAUGHAN, b. 20 July 1954 El Paso, Texas; m. Charles Wayne Flora 1975/ divorced 1987.

i. *Charles Lewis "Chad" Flora*, b. 16 September 1976 Baytown, Texas; m. Martha Romero 10 January 2003
ii. *Lindsay Anne Flora*, b. 2 May 1980 El Paso, Texas

EARL FRANCIS BROSNAHAN JR. AND JUNE THERESA MULLEN

MICHELLE THERESA BROSNAHAN, b. 12 October 1953; m. (now divorced) Jon Reese Pozgay.

i. *Whitney N. Pozgay*, b. 21 February 1981 Paradise Valley, Arizona
ii. *Jon Reese Pozgay*, b. 25 November 1985 Paradise Valley, Arizona; Brophy College Prep

EARL FRANCIS BROSNAHAN III, b. 25 January 1958 Kansas City, Missouri; m. Carol Best; Class of 1974, Pembroke Hill School, Kansas City, Missouri.

i. *Rachel Elizabeth Brosnahan*
ii. *Alec Francis Brosnahan*
iii. *Lydia Brosnahan*

ANNE MULLEN BROSNAHAN, b. 19 May 1959; m1 Steven Burstein 19 May 1984; m2 Nicholas Lee DiVita 24 April 1999 Montgomery, West Virginia.

RETA MOTTIN BROSNAHAN, b. 14 December 1960; m. Karl Saffo.

i. *Liza O'Flanagan Saffo*
ii. *Laith Saffo*

KATHERINE NOEL "KATE" BROSNAHAN, b. 24 December 1962 Kansas City, Missouri; University of New Mexico, 1986; 1991, left and took a job at Mademoiselle Magazine, as Senior Fashion editor/head of accessories; m. Andrew Spade (brother of actor/comedian, David Spade); January

1993, launched with husband "Kate Spade Handbags"; 1996, Council of Fashion Designers of America (CFDA) honored her handbags when exhibited at the Cooper Hewitt Museum for the first national design triennial; 2004, awarded three prestigious design awards; House Beautiful's Giants of Design Award for tastemaker, Bon Appetit's American Food and Entertaining Award for designer of the year; Elle Décor's Elle Décor International Design Award for bedding. She can be found throughout the website under "Kate Spade." She made an appearance as first guest judge of the season on Project Runway, led by Heidi Klum.

i.   *Beatrice Spade*

EVE MULLEN BROSNAHAN, b. 25 February 1965.

(DR.) LEGER NICHOLAS MOTTIN BROSNAHAN SR. AND (DR.) IRENE MAYSHIR TEOH

LEGER NICHOLAS "NICK" BROSNAHAN JR., b. 3 December 1969, Tokyo, Japan; Normal Community High School '88; Darmouth College '92; m. Anna Margarete Jaeckel, b. 8 January 1971 Pittsburgh, Pennsylvania; Lyon High School '88; Caltech '92.

i.   *Kellen Martin Brosnahan*, b. 7 February 2001 Mountain View, California

ii.   *Kyra Irene Brosnahan*, b. 28 October 2002 Mountain View, California

JENNIFER RU-CHIAO "JENNY" BROSNAHAN, b. 1 February 1973 Bloomington, Illinois; m. Kevin Joseph McIntyre on Saturday, June 2008, St. Joseph's on Capitol Hill, Washington. Msgr. Peter J. Vaghi performed the ceremony; served as deputy general counsel of the U.S. Department of Transportation in Washington; from 2003-2007, served in White House counsel's office as associate counsel to the president; graduated with a law degree from Harvard, magna cum laude.

MARY VIRGINIA BROSNAHAN AND (DR.) BENJAMIN D. MCCALLISTER

(DR.) BENJAMIN D. MCCALLISTER JR., M.D., b. 15 May 1957, Kansas City, Kansas; B.S., Stanford University; M.D., Vanderbilt Medical School, Nashville, Tennessee; joined Michigan Heart in 1991; interests include Non-Invasive Cardio Imaging, Valvular Heart Disease, Preventive Cardiology and Coronary Artery Disease; Echocardiography director, Michigan Heart, St. Joseph Mercy

Hospital, Ann Arbor, Michigan and for Chelsea Hospital and St. Mary Hospital in Livonia; President of Michigan Heart, PC ; member of Lipid Clinic; past director of Nuclear Cardiology and Exercise Testing, Michigan Heart; given numerous presentations and written research journal articles including Nuclear Cardiology, Stress Testing, Myocardial Infarction and Vascular Heart Disease; m. Elizabeth "Betsy" Meeker.

i. *Andrew Meeker McCallister*, b. 16 September 1990 Rochester, Minnesota
ii. *Ainsley Elizabeth McCallister*, b. 15 April 1992 Anne Arbor, Michigan
iii. *Reid Meeker McCallister*, b. 1 February 1995 Ann Arbor, Michigan
iv. *Miah Katherine McCallister*, b. 5 August 1999 Santa Rosa Guatemala

(DR.) SCOTT HORTON MCCALLISTER M.D., b. 9 February 1959 Honolulu, Hawaii; B.A., Kansas University; M.D. Kansas University Medical School; m. Julie.

i. *Magan Elizabeth McCallister*, b. 15 March 1994 Indianapolis, Indiana
ii. *Mathew Scott McCallister*, b. 21 January 1997 Phoenix, Arizona

JOHN GREGORY MCCALLISTER, b. 29 November 1962; Pembroke High School, Kansas City, Missouri; B.S., Harvard, Cum Laude; m. Caroline Lee Price Rhoden 2 September 1988; Associate Investor Banker, Salomon Brothers, London, England.

i. *Elena Swanson McCallister*, b. 27 March 1992 London, England
ii. *Maximillian Price McCallister*, b. 13 September 1994 Kansas City, Missouri

THOMAS MOTTIN MCCALLISTER, b. 28 December 1964 Rochester, Minnesota; Darmouth College; B.A., Dartmouth; L.L.B., Goldengate University; m. Gail McClelland Davis 29 May 1994.

i. *Margaret Ann McCallister*, b. 30 March 1997 Evanston, Illinois
ii. *Brady Thomas McCallister*, b. 6 April 1999 San Francisco, California
iii. *Katherine Olya McCallister*, b. 4 July 2002 St. Petersburg, Russia; adopted 4 July 2003

KATHERINE ANN MCCALLISTER, b. 13 April 1966 Rochester, Minnesota; B.A., Kansas University; M.B.A., Colorado University, Colorado ('92); m. Joseph Louis Cubba 5 July 2001 Boulder, Colorado;

managing director of strategic services at Lumedx Corporation; lived in Denver/Boulder area since graduating and moved in June to D.C. to be with her husband who works in missile defense with Northrop Grumman.

i. *Olivia Cubba*, b. 8 February 2005 Fairfax, Virginia

ROGER PAUL BROSNAHAN AND JILL ANN FARLEY

PAUL FARLEY BROSNAHAN, b. 14 September 1959; m. Jan Mackenzie Peterson.

i. *Machenazie Jill Brosnahan*, b. 30 June 1994
ii. *Roger Paul Brosnahan II*, b. 8 February 1996

CONNOR FRANCIS BROSNAHAN, b. 5 April 1963; m. Judith K. Ha.

i. *Brandon Patrick Brosnahan*, b. 1 August 2000
ii. *Liam Patrick Brosnahan*

TRACY TURNER VIVIAN BROSNAHAN, b. 28 November 1967; m1 ?; m2 Mitchell John Lobin.

i. *Ryan Mitchell Lobin*, b. 8 February 1998
ii. *John Turner Lobin*, b. 3 August 2001

PETER FARLEY BROSNAHAN, b. 2 November 1968 Rochester, Minnesota (by his birthmother, Laura Nordine?); childhood spent in Winona and White bear Lake, MN; Graduate of Hill Murray High School, St. Paul and Saint Mary's University, Winona; d. 22 January 2004 San Diego, California; Mass conducted at Sacred Heart, 360 Main St., Winona.

HELEN ROSE MOTTIN "NELLY" BROSNAHAN, b. 5 August 1970; m. Michael Steven Zauha.

i. *Anna Christine Zauha*, b. 28 September 2001
ii. *Eric Zauha*

LEE PATRICK BROSNAHAN, b. 13 November 1974; m. Christina Caroline Young.

i. *Lily Elizabeth Young Brosnahan*

HUGH BIHM BROSNAHAN, b. 7 February 1975; m1 ?; m2 Jennifer.

m1?:

i. *Angelice Brosnahan*, b. 2001

Hugh and Jennifer:

ii. *Dominic Brosnahan*
iii. *Abigail Brosnahan*

ROSEMARY O'BRENNAN AND WADE BAILEY PARKS

DUSTIN WADE PARKS, Angelo State University; location manager and production coordinator of El Camino Production.

CHRIS PARKS, b. 1990 Morse, Hansford County, Texas; senior champion of Hansford County; Pringle-Morse Consolidated Independent School District; band, running track, basketball and competing in UIL; class treasurer

CHASE BRIAN PARKS, b. 1989 Amarillo, Texas

ROBERTA KATHLEEN PIKE AND BERRY

PATRICK TIMOTHY BERRY, b. 16 October 1970, Smithville, Missouri; USN.

MICHAEL SEAN BERRY

ROBERT L. PIKE AND LISA A.

KATHLEEN L. PIKE

KEVIN R. PIKE, b. 1983 Leavenworth

JANET PIKE AND CARTER

CHUCK CARTER

AMANDA CARTER

CASSIE CARTER, m. Josh Jones

DENNIE RAE CORDOVA (BARKER)

Shawn Barker

PAUL SAMUEL FINCH AND NANCY LYN HADDAN

DAVID SPENCER FINCH, b. 15 May 1977, Colorado Springs, Colorado; 10 years, U.S.A.F.

MICHAEL PAUL FINCH, b. 12 December 1980, Craig, Colorado; U.S.A.F.

LYLE SPENCER FINCH AND CAREN LYNETTE BURST

ADAM CHARLES FINCH, b. 3 April 1986, Cheyenne, Wyoming; worked as a pipefitter apprentice with Western States Fire Protection; member of High Plains Canine Association; d. 18 December 2005, Cheyenne, Wyoming; cremation took place at Cheyenne Memorial Gardens by

Wiederspahn-Radomsky Chapel of the Chimes.

ELIAS KANE FINCH, b. 12 April 1988, Cheyenne, Wyoming

NORMAN CLIFTON HUNDSACKER AND MARGARET MARY BIEDERMAN

REX ROBERT SCHULTE, b. 11 September 1960, Coggon, Iowa; bapt. 2 April 1961, Coggon, Iowa; m1 Bobbie Whitney; m2 Paige Elkenberger; m3 Donna Petrie.

Rex and Bobbie:

i. *Angelina Kristina Schulte*
ii. *Casey James Schulte*
iii. *Joshua Robert Schulte*
iv. *Chris Orlando Schulte*

Rex and Donna:

v. *Bodie Schulte*
vi. *London Schulte*

ROBIN RENEE SCHULTE, b. 21 October 1961, Coggon, Iowa; m1 Randy L. Berry, June 1980; m2 Jim Crawford.

i. *Amanda Rae Berry*, b. 11 December 1980

RHETT RANDALL SCHULTE, b. 17 July 1963, Coggon, Iowa; m1 Ann;

m2 Rita; m3 Heldelisa Guzman 4 July 2005 (no children).

Rhett and Ann:

i. *Vanessa Schulte*
ii. *Jeanine Schulte*
iii. *Kristen Schulte*

RHONDA RAE SCHULTE, b. 5 November 1964, Coggon, Iowa; m1 Steven Richard Sr.; m2 Bowers.

Rhonda and Steven:

i. *Steven Richard Jr.*

RHAFE RANDOM SCHULTE, b. 4 October 1967, Coggon, Iowa; d. 28 November 1988

NORMAN CLIFTON HUNDSACKER AND CATHERINE ANN PILLARELLI

MICHAEL CLIFTON SCHULTE, b. 4 August 1980

LEE E. HATTOK m1 JANET

PAUL J. HATTOK

NANCY HATTOK

JOHN HATTOK

LEE HATTOK, m. Ann

LEE E. HATTOK M2
ANN

Brian Hattok

FRANCIS WILLIAM HATTOK AND
SANDRA BETH MOOREHEAD

JOHN F. HATTOK, b. 1978; m. Ann; twins (b and g), Linsey

DONNA JEAN HATTOK AND
BOB WOOD

Connie Wood

Debbie Wood

DONNA JEAN HATTOK AND
JESUS RIOG

Renee Riog

MAXINE MAE HATTOK AND
ROBERT W. TUCKER

Ronnie Tucker

Rebecca Tucker

Richard Tucker

Misty Tucker

Robert Tucker

CARLEEN MARIE BARRY

James P. Barry

Margaret C. Barry

Sheldon C. Barry

Donielle Elizabeth Barry

COLLEEN BARRY AND
MICHAEL J. WAITE

ZACHARY D. (PAIGE) WAITE, graduated from Leavenworth Sr. High 2003; graduated A.F. Basic Training, Honor Grad, 10 March 2009; serving Osan AFB, Korea.

DOROTHY ANN HATTOK AND
JACK MESSER

JEREMY MESSER, military vet, hospitalized at Walter Reed, medically discharged.

www.ingramcontent.com/pod-product-compliance
Lightning Source LLC
Chambersburg PA
CBHW030357290526
45785CB00004B/1788